Of Miracles

Of Miracles

David Hume

Furnished with an Introduction and Notes by

Antony Flew

Open Court
La Salle, Illinois

Library of Congress Cataloging in Publication Data
Hume, David, 1711-1776
Of miracles.

(Open Court classics)
Bibliography: p.
1. Miracles — Early works to 1800. 2. Hume, David, 1711–1776 — Views on miracles. I. Title.
B1499.M5H85   1985   210   85-11410
ISBN 0-8126-9072-9
ISBN 0-912050-72-1 (pbk.)

CU: OpenCourt / OCPublish / Hume / CopyrtPg
copyright page for Open Court Hume: On Miracles
1st run 9/3/87 tvm
Paul Baker Typography, Inc.
fonts 34,36,569,996

Introduction

by Antony Flew

1. 'Of Miracles' in Hume's work as a whole

David Hume was born in 1711 and died in 1776, the year of the American Declaration of Independence. (It was an event which he had long foreseen, and at once welcomed.) Hume's treatment 'Of Miracles' (1748) quickly became, and long remained, the most scandalous and controversial of all his works. In more recent years it has often been neglected, even by those to whom its message is most relevant. Many too of those who have studied it have, through tearing it out of context, failed fully to understand and come to terms with both its strength and its weaknesses. The purpose of the present Introduction is to provide that context, to indicate the true direction and the formidable force of Hume's argument, and to remedy those weaknesses.

Hume's first work, published anonymously before the author had turned thirty, was *A Treatise of Human Nature* (1739–40). The title is significant. For although the *Treatise* is now by common consent allowed to be one of the great classics of philosophy, by Hume himself it was seen—to employ a distinction not current in his day—not as an exotic exercise in purely professional philosophizing, but rather as a contribution to psychology and to other empirical human studies. According to the rueful retrospect of *My Own Life*, this "juvenile work ... fell *dead-born from the press.*" Not permitting himself to be for long discouraged, Hume soon produced a second book, the two-volume *Essays, Moral and Political.*

In 1748 this was followed by the book eventually entitled *An Enquiry concerning Human Understanding.* In 1752 this first *Enquiry* was followed by a second, *An Enquiry Concerning the Principles of Morals*—as well as by the more immediately successful *Political Discourses.* In the same year, having been appointed Librarian to the Faculty of Advocates in Edinburgh, Hume started work on his *History of England.* This quickly became standard. It continued to go into fresh editions for over a century. The catalogue of the British Museum Library still lists the author as simply: "Hume, David, the historian."

The first *Enquiry* was an investigation in the genre of John Locke's *Essay concerning Human Understanding* (1690), a genre in which, later in Hume's century, both works were to be joined by the three great *Critiques* of Immanuel Kant (1724–1804). In an introductory 'Epistle to the Reader' Locke tells us how one day he and some friends, discussing unspecified grand philosophical issues, found themselves completely "at a stand" (deadlocked). It appeared that no progress would or could be achieved until and unless they first discovered what "our understanding were, or were not, fitted to deal with", what it is and is not possible for creatures such as we to find out and to know.

It is to this most fundamental investigation that both Locke's *Essay* and Hume's first *Enquiry* are devoted, while Hume's treatment 'Of Miracles' is essential to the whole project of that *Enquiry*. It was therefore originally published as Section X of *An Enquiry concerning Human Understanding*. But during the nineteenth century, in the edition of Hume's *Essays Literary Moral and Political* in Sir John Lubbock's best-selling Hundred Books series, both this Section X and the subsequent Section XI are excised, to appear only in a reluctant Appendix. This has a remarkable initial note beginning: "These essays are generally omitted in popular editions of the writings of Hume." In our own century, in what has been and is the most widely used edition of the first and second *Enquiries* together, both these sections are included in their proper places. Nevertheless the Editor in his Introduction dismisses them as an irrelevant and offensive addition, to be explained only by reference to "Hume's ambition to disturb 'the zealots' at all costs." (In *My Own Life* Hume had lamented that his *Treatise* had not achieved "such distinction as even to excite a murmer among the zealots"—by which he meant those who would be shocked by his irreligion.)

2. Hume's aim in 'Of Miracles'

This brings us to the second point which the reader of 'Of Miracles' must always hold firmly in mind. It is that Hume's prime concern here is with knowledge, and hence with evidence rather than fact. He is not asking whether any miracles have occurred or do occur—though he makes it plain that as a "wise man ... who proportions his belief to the evidence", he is himself quite certain that they have not, and do not. Instead he is asking whether and, if so, how—even supposing that a miracle had occurred—we could know, repeat *know*, that it had. Most especially he is asking—and urging that we must answer in the negative—a more particular question: "whether a miracle can [ever] be proved, so as to be the foundation of a system of religion".

3. Miracles as evidence of true revelation

The third matter to master before starting to study 'Of Miracles' is the reason why this more particular question is both of great intrinsic importance and indispensably relevant to the whole project of this first *Enquiry*. In a nutshell, it is that there would seem to be no other way of showing that the Christian, or any rival candidate, is a genuine Revelation of the true God. To serve as the key term in such a demonstration, the word 'miracle' has to be construed (as both Hume himself and all his contemporary opponents did construe it) in a very strong sense. It must involve an overriding of a law of nature, a doing of what is known to be naturally impossible by a Power which is, by this very overriding, shown to be Supernatural and Supreme.

Only if this is given can the occurrence of a miracle under the auspices of some particular system of belief constitute an inexpugnable Divine endorsement of that system. Without appreciating the rationality and the straightforwardness of this approach to the settling of disputes between the protagonists of incompatible sets of religious beliefs, we cannot hope to understand either Hume's insistence that the miracle stories of rival religions must be assessed as not merely different but contrary, or the delighted attention which he gives to the then recent Affair of the Abbé Paris. It was precisely and only because both the Jansenists and the Jesuits did accept these principles that both parties were so keen to show, the one that miracles had occurred at that cleric's tomb, and the other that they had not.

In Section X, and in the following Section XI, Hume deploys his case against the traditional reasoned apologetic for Christianity. He tries to discredit—and, I believe, succeeds in discrediting—the whole bold attempt. Its first stage consisted in labouring to establish, by appealing only to natural reason and common experience, the existence and certain minimal characteristics of God. The second stage tried to supplement this inevitably somewhat sketchy religion of nature with a more abundant Revelation.

This programme, in its characteristically eighteenth century form, achieved archetypal fulfilment in Archdeacon William Paley's *Natural Theology* (London, 1802) and in the same author's *Evidences of Christianity* (London, 1794). Here the weight of the first part of the case was borne mainly by the Argument to Design: if from a watch we may infer a watchmaker, then surely the orderliness of the Universe entitles us to infer, by parity of reasoning, a Universe-Maker?

It is this argument which Hume attacks in Section XI, and more extensively in his posthumous masterpiece—revised finally on his deathbed—the *Dialogues concerning Natural Religion* (1779). All the other arguments are dismissed in very short order in Section XII (iii), as well as (rather less briefly) in the later work. The second part of the traditional case rested upon the claim that there is ample historical evidence to show that the Biblical miracles, including crucially the physical resurrection of Jesus bar Joseph, did in fact occur; and that this in turn proved the crucial Christian claims.

The general validity of this two-stage apologetic, although not that of any particular putative proof of Natural Theology, was defined in 1870 by the First Vatican Council as itself a dogma necessary to salvation. However, we have to notice that since the Second Vatican Council touched off the progressive Protestantization of the Roman Church this defined dogma appears to have become one item rather rarely picked by those professing Catholics who insist on choosing out of the historic deposit of the Faith their own individual anthologies of credibility. The relevant canon dealing with the second stage neither hesitates nor compromises: "If anyone shall say ... that miracles can never be known for certain, or that the divine origin of the Christian religion cannot properly be proved by them: let him be anathema."

There are many today who, while continuing to claim the Christian name, feel forced to abandon that strong conception of the miraculous, and indeed the whole rational apologetic for which it provides a crucial term. This puts them in a doubly desperate position. In the first place, they can scarcely hope to develop what too often they do not even bother to seek: any better alternative way of trying to show that their faith is reasonable. In the second place, one particular miracle story—that of what myriads of old-fashioned Easter sermons have insisted must be the miracle of miracles—is not merely evidence for the authenticity of the Christian Revelation, but is also integral to it. It is the very heart and essence of the Gospel message that the second person of the Trinity became man: that He was born of woman, if not necessarily of a virgin; that He preached the word of his Father in the Galilee; that He was crucified, dead and buried; *and that He rose again on the third day.* It was not, therefore, any wanton or gratuitous desire to shock which led Hume to introduce his factitious legend of the Resurrection of Elizabeth the Great. It was, rather, the need to press his argument home.

4. Miracles and laws of nature

That argument takes off from the observation that there cannot but be a conflict, even a contradiction, within any suitably comprehensive case for saying that a miracle has actually occurred. Such a case has to show: first, that the supposed laws, of which the actual occurrence of the putatively miraculous events would constitute an overriding, do in fact obtain; and, second, that the overridings have in fact occurred.

All evidence for the first proposition, however, is at the same time evidence against the second; and the other way about. For to say that a law of nature obtains just is to say that it is (not logically or apriori, but naturally and practically) impossible for any events to occur such that these events would by their occurring falsify the universal and nomological (law-stating) proposition which expresses that law of nature. Thus, to show that a law of nature obtains just is to show that the occurrence of exceptions is naturally impossible; while to show that even one 'exception' has occurred would be to show that that law, at least in that formulation, did not obtain.

This conflict or contradiction can be resolved; but only at what must here be an unacceptable price. Certainly it is open to spokespersons for the miraculous to claim that their alleged revelations provide them with the necessary criteria. These are the criteria which they need for distinguishing between, on the one hand, those exceptions which as overridings by a Power above and outside Nature do not constitute true falsifications of the supposed laws of nature, and on the other hand, those exceptions' which are truly falsifying—and hence call for further and hopefully more successful creative work by scientists.

It is, or ought to be, obvious why such a resolution cannot be accepted by anyone committed to the traditional apologetic. If the occurrence of a miracle is to serve as an endorsement of a candidate revelation, then we have to excogitate some means entirely independent of that putative revelation by which this guarantee itself can be recognized. A parallel objection arises if, with what has become a fasionable school in theology, you urge that miracles are not really overridings but signs. If a sign is to signify to the unbeliever, then there has to be some means independent of the doctrinal system itself whereby the signs may be identified as such, and their significations understood.

5. Two weaknesses in Hume's argument

Hume's general presentation of his argument in Part I of Section X has two serious but remediable weaknesses. The first of these arises because he has not yet altogether abandoned one hope cherished at the time of the *Treatise.* This is the hope of producing a kind of mechanics of consciousness, with principles of the association of ideas relating moments of consciousness in something like the way in which the principles of classical mechanics related the "hard, massy and impenetrable" billiard balls of atomic theory. The second is that given his distinctive account of causal necessity, and the consequent pure regularity analysis of laws of nature, Hume cannot himself provide for any substantial distinction between the extremely unusual and the authentically miraculous.

To the first of these weaknesses the best response is: to begin by appreciating what Hume was understandably, if no doubt misguidedly, trying to do; next perhaps to smile at his efforts; and finally to pass on. Take, as an example of his laughably literalistic and plonkingly quantitative interpretation of the weighing of evidence, this statement: "A hundred instances or experiments on one side, and fifty on another, afford a doubtful expectation of any event. . . . In all cases, we must balance the opposite experiments, when they are opposite, and deduct the smaller number from the greater, in order to know the exact force of the superior evidence."

The second weakness is much more serious, and much less easily remedied. Yet it is one not likely to be noticed by anyone who reads 'Of Miracles' out of context. For Hume certainly does not make explicit, and maybe he never even noticed, the upsetting implications for his present argument of earlier contentions. Thus, having considered testimony for the unusual and the marvellous, Hume continues: "But in order to increase the probability against the testimony of witnesses, let us suppose, that the fact, which they affirm, instead of being only marvellous, is really miraculous. . . ." He then proceeds to define 'a miracle' as "a violation of the laws of nature"; or, more "accurately," as *"a transgression of a law of nature by a particular volition of the Deity."*

As a controversial move this cannot be faulted. For in this definition Hume is providing precisely and only what his chosen opponents want and need: without such a strong notion requiring the particular intervention of a Power above and greater than Nature, they could not get their act on the road at all. But Hume appears to have forgotten that he has earlier argued that there are

10

no natural necessities and no natural impossibilities: there is only logical necessity and logical impossibility. In his view, however, even these genuine necessities and genuine impossibilities do not characterize the non-linguistic world. For all that we could know apriori, anything might be the cause of anything, while, as Hume urged in the *Treatise* but not in any later work, it is even conceivable that events might occur without any causes at all.

Among the further consequences of these radical contentions, one is that laws of nature, in so far as they are descriptive of the phenomena to which they apply, state only that ongoings of one particular sort will in fact always be accompanied by ongoings of another particular sort. They do not state, neither do they imply, that once an event of the one sort has occurred, it must be impossible by any human or other natural force to prevent the occurrence of an event of the other sort. Laws of nature, therefore, as thus understood—or rather misunderstood—by Hume could provide no purchase for any overriding manifestations of the definitionally Supernatural Deity.

Again, Humean causes are only followed by, they do not bring about, their effects: the occurrence of the cause event, that is, does not either make necessary the occurrence of the effect event or make impossible its non-occurrence. The only necessity involved, according to Hume, is a muddled notion in us as we think about causes. It is a matter of our feeling the force of habitual associations of corresponding ideas, and projecting this muddle out onto realities among which there are to be found no necessities of any kind.

It is not possible here to essay a comprehensive and constructive critique of Hume's accounts of causation and of laws of nature. Sufficient indeed for the moment to have brought out their relevant consequences, and in that way to have suggested that for us the most promising course is to proceed as if we had never heard of Hume's denials of natural necessity and natural impossibility. That, after all, is how in our present context Hume himself proceeded!

6. Evaluating historical evidence

So far we have followed Hume in concentrating upon the question of proving a miracle "so as to be the foundation of a system of religion." But the argument expounded in Part I has a far more extensive application. It is, he claims there, "a decisive argument . . . which must at least silence the most arrogant bigotry and superstition, and free us from their impertinent solicitations . . . an argument which . . . will . . . with the wise and learned, be an everlasting check to all kinds of superstitious delusion. . . ."

It is sometimes thought that there is no more to this "everlasting check" than a trite reminder that, because the occurrence of a miracle must be very improbable, it needs to be quite exceptionally well evidenced. But C. S. Peirce, who seems never to have exploited it fully, had the vital clue in his hands when he remarked: "The whole of modern 'higher criticism' of ancient history in general . . . is based upon the same logic as is used by Hume." The truth is that this section of 'Of Miracles' belongs not only to the philosophy of religion but also to the philosophy of history. It has too a major bearing on the philosophy of science in general, and, in particular, on that of the would-be science of parapsychology.

What, with some lapses and hesitations, Hume is contending is that the criteria by which we must assess historical testimony, and the general presumptions which alone allow us to interpret the detritus of the past as historical evidence, must inevitably rule out any possibility of establishing definitively, upon purely historical evidence, that some genuinely miraculous event has occurred.

His fundamental theses are: first, that the detritus of the past cannot be construed as any sort of historical evidence unless we presume that the same basic regularities obtained then as obtain today; and second, that in trying as best he may to determine what actually happened, the historian has to employ as criteria all his present knowledge and presumed knowledge of what is probable or improbable, possible or impossible. In his *Treatise* (II [iii] 1), Hume had argued that it is only upon such presumptions that we can justify even the basic conclusion that certain kinds of ink marks on old pieces of paper constitute testimonial evidence. Earlier in his first *Enquiry* (VIII [i]), he had urged the inescapable importance of having such criteria; while, in what was originally a footnote to 'Of Miracles', he quotes with approval the reasoning of the famous physician De Sylva in the contested case of a Mademoiselle Thibaut. "It was impossible she could have been so ill as was proved by witnesses, because it was impossible that she could, in so short a time, have recovered so perfectly as he found her."

Two serious faults in Hume's presentation may obscure the force and soundness of De Sylva's reasoning and the fact that this sort of application of canons to evidence is absolutely essential to the very possibility of critical history. The first is that, contrary to his own sceptical principles, Hume tends to take it for granted that what in his own day he and all his fellow persons of sense firmly believed about the order of nature constituted not just well-grounded, yet always humanly fallible opinion, but the definitive and incorrigible last word. He is thus betrayed into rejecting as downright impossible certain reported phenomena which the progress of abnormal psychology and psychosomatic medicine has since shown to have been perfectly possible.

For instance: like other eighteenth century sceptics Hume makes much of the miracles supposedly wrought in Egypt by the soldier Emperor Vespasian, suggesting, if never outright stating, that the evidence in this case is far and away stronger than that for any of the miracle stories of the *New Testament*. Suppose that we are so conscientiously curious as to refer to the accounts given in the Roman historians Suetonius and Tacitus. We find that, according to Suetonius, when the Emperor was in Egypt "two labourers, one blind and the other lame, approached him, begging to be healed; apparently the god Serapis had promised them in a dream that if Vespasian would consent to spit in the blind man's eye and touch the lame man's leg with his heel, both would be cured." According to the longer account in Tacitus (in which the lame man becomes a man with a withered hand), Vespasian "asked the

doctors for an opinion whether blindness and
atrophy of this sort were curable by human means.
The doctors were eloquent about the various
possibilities: the blind man's vision was not
completely destroyed, and, if certain impediments
were removed, his sight would return; the other
man's limb had been dislocated, but could be put
right by correct treatment. . . . Anyway, if a cure
were effected, the credit would go to the ruler; if it
failed, the poor wretches would have to bear the
ridicule." Both historians go on to tell us that
Vespasian did what he had been asked to do,
and that the two patients were in consequence
cured.

So, given those medical reports insisting on the
absence of any gross organic lesions, and in the
light of what has since been learned about
psychosomatic possibilities, we now have to say:
not that Vespasian did after all perform two
miracles of healing during his Egyptian tour, and
that this is something which we now know on
sound historical grounds; but that what Hume
dismissed as something which could not have
occurred, because its occurrence would have been
miraculous, in fact did occur, but was not
miraculous. Our reason for saying that the cures
were indeed effected is at the same time our reason
for saying that they were not miraculous.

Before moving on to the second fault in Hume's
presentation let us notice another case equally
Classical but much less disputed. In Herodotus,
"the father of critical history", we read that at the
time of the Pharaoh Necho II (about 600 B.C.)
Phoenician sailors claimed to have circumnavigated
Africa. They said that they had sailed South down

what we call the Red Sea and arrived at the
Mediterranean coast of Egypt nearly three years
later. The interesting thing for us is their report
that during the voyage the position of the sun
shifted from the South to the North, and back
again. Herodotus, recording that they said this,
states that he himself does not believe what they
said. He had two good reasons for disbelief: first,
he knew that Phoenician and other sailors were apt
to tell tall tales; and second, he took it that he
knew that what the sailors reported was
impossible. Herodotus therefore had good reason to
dismiss this story, and did dismiss it.

But for us, what was for Herodotus an excellent
reason for incredulity is the decisive ground for
believing that Phoenicians did in fact
circumnavigate Africa at this time. They could
scarcely have got this thing about the changing
relative position of the Sun right unless they had
actually made the voyage which they said they had
made. Both Herodotus and the successors who have
on this point put him right were employing the
same sound historical methods, the only methods
possible for the critical historian.

Both he and we, that is, are and cannot but be
committed, in interpreting and assessing the
detritus of the past as historical evidence, to
appealing to all that we know or think we know
about what is probable or improbable, possible or
impossible. Thus Herodotus, in trying to interpret
the evidence of the Phoenicians, rightly appealed to
what he knew, or thought he knew, about
astronomy and geography. We, following exactly
the same fundamental principles of historical
reconstruction, but having the advantage over him

of knowing more about astronomy and geography, reach different conclusions, albeit by fundamentally the same methods.

The second serious fault in Hume's presentation arises from the inadequacies of his accounts of causation and of laws of nature, inadequacies briefly indicated in Section 4 above. This second fault is that Hume is unable to make clear why, if we are confronted with what appears to be overwhelmingly strong evidence for some occurrence believed to be impossible, it must almost if not quite always be wrong to conclude that that event did after all occur rather than that we have been mistaken in believing it impossible. Hume does concede that circumstances could arise in which we ought to admit the occurrence, and therefore reject the proposition which previously we had believed to express a law of nature. But the rationale supplied is quite inadequate.

Suppose, Hume writes, that "all authors in all languages, agree that from the first of January, 1600, there was a total darkness over the whole earth for eight days; suppose that the tradition of this extraordinary event is still strong and lively among the people; that all travellers who return from foreign countries bring us accounts of the same tradition without the least variation or contradiction—it is evident that our present philosophers, instead of doubting the fact, ought to receive it as certain and ought to search for the causes whence it might be derived."

A more manageably plausible example can be produced by supposing that European astronomers, when word first reached them of the eclipse observations made centuries earlier in China, had been committed to a theory precluding the occurrence of any eclipses visible at any of the times or in any of the places listed in the Chinese records. Then, if there was no independent reason for suspecting the truth of those Chinese observations—no state ideology, for instance, to be supported by the occurrence of eclipses in those places and at those times—it would surely have been right for the European astronomers, after admitting that they seemed to have been on the wrong track, to get back to their theoretical drawing boards. Our past philosophers, as Hume might have put it, instead of doubting the Chinese facts, ought to have received them as certain, and ought to have searched for the causes whence they might have been derived.

The crux here is again a matter of actual and possible evidence. The historical propositions, the propositions stating that an eclipse was visible in such and such a place at such and such a time, are all singular and in the past tense. It is always and necessarily too late now for any direct verification or falsification. If we are ever to discover what actually happened, this can only be by finding something present which can be interpreted as evidence, and by assessing what and how much that available evidence shows.

It is altogether different with nomological propositions; propositions, that is, which state that causal connections or laws of nature obtain; and which necessarily imply something about practical necessity and practical impossibility. Nomological propositions are open and general and can, at least in principle, be tested for truth or falsity at any time or in any place. Precisely that is why it is reasonable and right for the critical historian to employ all available confirmed nomologicals as canons of exclusion, ruling out many conceivable and even sometimes seemingly well-evidenced occurrences as practically impossible. Yet in doing this our historians should always be aware that steady advances in our knowledge of nomologicals, and occasional upsets revealing that what we had believed to constitute such knowledge was not, may demand historical reassessments—as in the cases of the supposed miracles of Vespasian and the alleged Phoenician circumnavigation of Africa.

7. Miracles of parapsychology

At the very beginning of 'Of Miracles' Hume, as we have seen, expresses the confident hope that he is about to offer "an argument which . . . will . . . with the wise and learned, be an everlasting check to all kinds of superstitious delusion. . . ." Certainly he would have rated the claims of parapsychology among those "impertinent solicitations" from which he was promising to free us. Nor is there any doubt but that his argument is relevant. For parapsychology is the would-be science of the paranormal, while that in turn is implicitly defined in terms of incompatibility with various normal beliefs about the practically impossible.

These putative phenomena are best labelled, in a studiously theory-neutral way, the psi-phenomena. This genus is then divided into two species: psi-gamma; and psi-kappa. The former includes all varieties of what used to be called Extrasensory Perception (ESP): telepathy, that is to say, and clairvoyance, whether retrocognitive, simultaneous, or precognitive. The latter is, in effect, a more non-committal word for psychokinesis (etymologically, 'movement by the mind').

It is usual to maintain that the phenomena, or alleged phenomena, of parapsychology are, or would be, non-physical or even outright incompatible with physics. But what such psi-phenomena are or would be incompatible with is not, or not primarily, any particular named law of physics: Boyle's Law, or what have you. Instead they do or would—as Hume liked to say—violate something far more universal and fundamental. What rules them out as impossible are some of what have been identified as our "basic limiting principles"; principles which together constitute a framework for all our everyday thinking about, and investigation of, human affairs; and principles which are continually being verified by our discoveries.

If, for instance, official secret information gets out from a government office, then the security people try to think of every possible channel of leakage; and what never appears on the check lists of such practical persons is psi-gamma. When similarly there has been an explosion in a power station or other industrial plant, then the investigators move in. At no stage will they entertain any suggestion that no one and nothing touched anything, that the explosion was triggered by some conscious or unconscious exercise of psi-kappa. Nor shall we expect them to turn up any reason for thinking that their, and our, framework assumptions were here mistaken.

It is, therefore, not surprising that sceptics should have redeployed Hume's argument as a challenge to the parapsychologists. In 1955, for instance, *Science* published a paper by G. R. Price doing precisely that (Vol. CXXII, No. 3165, pp. 359–367). This brought a strong response from Paul Meehl and Michael Scriven: "Price is in exactly the position of a man who might have insisted that Michelson and Morley were liars because the evidence for the physical theory of that time was stronger than that for the veracity of the experimenters."

It is most important to appreciate the reasons why this is not so. The first reason is that the Michelson-Morley experiment was *not* one member of a long series including many impressively disillusioning examples of fraud and self-deception. By contrast the history of parapsychology is full both of supposedly decisive demonstrations and of investigators of allegedly impeccable integrity, which and who have later been exposed as fraudulent. Testimony in this area would appear to suffer all the corruptions believed by Hume to afflict the foundations of "systems of religion". For the issues are, in a more modern terminology, ideologically sensitive.

Second, there was in the Michelson-Morley case no reason at the time—nor has any such reason emerged since—to suspect that the experiment would not be repeatable, and repeated; as well as confirmed indirectly by other experiments similarly repeatable and repeated. But in parapsychology there are no regularly and reliably repeatable experiments; indeed there is no regularly and reliably repeatable demonstration of the reality of any psi-phenomenon. (This is, incidentally, the reason why the Parapsychological Association ought never to have been permitted to affiliate to the American Association for the Advancement of Science, and should be expelled forthwith; unless affiliation is intended to be a tribute to scientific intentions rather than scientific achievement.)

Third, there is no even halfway plausible theory to account for the occurrence of psi-phenomena. This deficiency bears on the question of scientific status in two ways. For a theory which related the putative psi-phenomena to something else less contentious would tend both to probabilify their actual occurrence and to explain why they do thus indeed occur. Here we have the third reason why to refuse to accept the reality of such phenomena is not on all fours with dismissing the result of the Michelson-Morley experiment. For, even if no one then was ready immediately with an alternative theory, still in that case there was no good reason to fear that such a theory could not be produced. But, in the case of parapsychology now, our investigators have had a hundred years for theoretical cogitation; from which labours they have as yet brought forth nothing.

These three objections reinforce one another. So, until and unless someone comes up with a reliably and regularly repeatable demonstration of some psi-phenomenon, we shall continue to have no sufficient reason to abandon any of those basic limiting principles which support the conclusions that all such phenomena are in fact impossible. The most generous verdict which can be brought in by a jury of wise men, who, as good Humeans proportion their belief to the evidence—and would not even this verdict be too generous?—is a damping, and appropriately Scottish, 'Not proven!'

PREFATORY NOTE

The text is exactly as Hume wrote it, except for the following modifications.

Three of Hume's footnotes to 'Of Miracles' are so substantial and readable that I have incorporated them into the main body of the text. In each case where this has been done, it is indicated in my own notes at the back. All the contents of Hume's notes are included in either the text or my notes.

A few spellings have been modernized. I have changed 'cotemporary' to 'contemporary', 'Arragon' to 'Aragon', 'substract' to 'subtract', and 'encrease' to 'increase'.

Antony Flew

Part 1.

There is, in Dr. Tillotson's writings, an argument against the *real presence*, which is as concise, and elegant, and strong as any argument can possibly be supposed against a doctrine, so little worthy of a serious refutation.[1] It is acknowledged on all hands, says that learned prelate, that the authority, either of the scripture or of tradition, is founded merely in the testimony of the apostles, who were eye-witnesses to those miracles of our Saviour, by which he proved his divine mission. Our evidence, then, for the truth of the *Christian* religion is less than the evidence for the truth of our senses; because, even in the first authors of our religion, it was no greater; and it is evident it must diminish in passing from them to their disciples; nor can any one rest such confidence in their testimony, as in the immediate object of his senses. But a weaker evidence can never destroy a stronger; and therefore, were the doctrine of the real presence ever so clearly revealed in scripture, it were directly contrary to the rules of just reasoning to give our assent to it. It contradicts sense, though both the scripture and tradition, on which it is supposed to be built, carry not such evidence with them as sense; when they are considered merely as external evidences, and are not brought home to every one's breast, by the immediate operation of the Holy Spirit.

Nothing is so convenient as a decisive argument of this kind, which must at least *silence* the most arrogant bigotry and superstition, and free us from their impertinent solicitations. I flatter myself, that I have discovered an argument of a like nature which, if just, will, with the wise and learned, be an everlasting check to all kinds of superstitious delusion, and, consequently, will be useful as long as the world endures; for so long, I presume, will the accounts of miracles and prodigies be found in all history, sacred and profane.

Though experience be our only guide in reasoning concerning matters of fact, it must be acknowledged that this guide is not altogether infallible, but in some cases is apt to lead us into errors. One who in our climate should expect better weather in any week of June than in one of December would reason justly and conformably to experience; but it is certain that he may happen, in the event, to find himself mistaken. However, we may observe that in such a case he would have no cause to complain of experience; because it commonly informs us beforehand of the uncertainty, by that contrariety of events which we may learn from a diligent observation. All effects follow not with like certainty from their supposed causes. Some events are found, in all countries and all ages, to have been constantly conjoined

together; others are found to have been more
variable, and sometimes to disappoint our
expectations, so that in our reasonings concerning
matter of fact there are all imaginable degrees of
assurance, from the highest certainty to the lowest
species of moral evidence.[2]

A wise man, therefore, proportions his belief to
the evidence. In such conclusions as are founded on
an infallible experience, he expects the event with
the last degree of assurance, and regards his past
experience as a full *proof* of the future existence of
that event. In other cases, he proceeds with more
caution: He weighs the opposite experiments:[3] He
considers which side is supported by the greater
number of experiments: to that side he inclines,
with doubt and hesitation; and when at last he
fixes his judgement, the evidence exceeds not what
we properly call *probability*. All probability, then,
supposes an opposition of experiments and
observations, where the one side is found to
overbalance the other, and to produce a degree of
evidence, proportioned to the superiority. A
hundred instances or experiments on one side, and
fifty on another, afford a doubtful expectation of
any event; though a hundred uniform experiments,
with only one that is contradictory, reasonably
beget a pretty strong degree of assurance. In all
cases, we must balance the opposite experiments,
where they are opposite, and deduct the smaller
number from the greater, in order to know the
exact force of the superior evidence.

To apply these principles to a particular
instance; we may observe, that there is no species
of reasoning more common, more useful, and even
necessary to human life, than that which is derived

from the testimony of men, and the reports of
eye-witnesses and spectators. This species of
reasoning, perhaps, one may deny to be founded on
the relation of cause and effect. I shall not dispute
about a word. It will be sufficient to observe that
our assurance in any argument of this kind is
derived from no other principle than our
observation of the veracity of human testimony,
and of the usual conformity of facts to the reports
of witnesses. It being a general maxim, that no
objects have any discoverable connexion together,
and that all the inferences, which we can draw
from one to another, are founded merely on our
experience of their constant and regular
conjunction; it is evident, that we ought not to
make an exception to this maxim in favour of
human testimony, whose connexion with any event
seems, in itself, as little necessary as any other.
Were not the memory tenacious to a certain degree;
had not men commonly an inclination to truth and
a principle of probity; were they not sensible to
shame, when detected in a falsehood: Were not
these, I say, discovered by *experience* to be
qualities, inherent in human nature, we should
never repose the least confidence in human
testimony. A man delirious, or noted for falsehood
and villany, has no manner of authority with us.

And as the evidence, derived from witnesses and
human testimony, is founded on past experience, so
it varies with the experience, and is regarded either
as a *proof* or a *probability*, according as the
conjunction between any particular kind of report
and any kind of object has been found to be
constant or variable. There are a number of
circumstances to be taken into consideration in all

judgements of this kind; and the ultimate standard, by which we determine all disputes, that may arise concerning them, is always derived from experience and observation. Where this experience is not entirely uniform on any side, it is attended with an unavoidable contrariety in our judgements, and with the same opposition and mutual destruction of argument as in every other kind of evidence. We frequently hesitate concerning the reports of others. We balance the opposite circumstances, which cause any doubt or uncertainty; and when we discover a superiority on any side, we incline to it; but still with a diminution of assurance, in proportion to the force of its antagonist.

This contrariety of evidence, in the present case, may be derived from several different causes; from the opposition of contrary testimony; from the character or number of the witnesses; from the manner of their delivering their testimony; or from the union of all these circumstances. We entertain a suspicion concerning any matter of fact, when the witnesses contradict each other; when they are but few, or of a doubtful character; when they have an interest in what they affirm; when they deliver their testimony with hesitation, or on the contrary, with too violent asseverations. There are many other particulars of the same kind, which may diminish or destroy the force of any argument, derived from human testimony.

Suppose, for instance, that the fact, which the testimony endeavours to establish, partakes of the extraordinary and the marvellous; in that case, the evidence, resulting from the testimony, admits of a diminution, greater or less, in proportion as the fact is more or less unusual. The reason why we place any credit in witnesses and historians, is not derived from any *connexion*, which we perceive *a priori*, between testimony and reality, but because we are accustomed to find a conformity between them. But when the fact attested is such a one as has seldom fallen under our observation, here is a contest of two opposite experiences; of which the one destroys the other, as far as its force goes, and the superior can only operate on the mind by the force, which remains. The very same principle of experience, which gives us a certain degree of assurance in the testimony of witnesses, gives us also, in this case, another degree of assurance against the fact, which they endeavour to establish; from which contradiction there necessarily arises a counterpoize, and mutual destruction of belief and authority.

I should not believe such a story were it told me by Cato, was a proverbial saying in Rome, even during the lifetime of that philosophical patriot.[4] The incredibility of a fact, it was allowed, might invalidate so great an authority.

The Indian prince, who refused to believe the first relations concerning the effects of frost, reasoned justly; and it naturally required very strong testimony to engage his assent to facts, that arose from a state of nature, with which he was unacquainted, and which bore so little analogy to those events, of which he had had constant and uniform experience. Though they were not contrary to his experience, they were not conformable to it.[5]

No Indian, it is evident, could have experience that water did not freeze in cold climates. This is placing nature in a situation quite unknown to him; and it is impossible for him to tell *a priori* what will result from it. It is making a new experiment, the consequence of which is always uncertain. One may sometimes conjecture from analogy what will follow; but still this is but conjecture. And it must be confessed that, in the present case of freezing, the event follows contrary to the rules of analogy, and is such as a rational Indian would not look for. The operations of cold upon water are not gradual, according to the degrees of cold; but whenever it comes to the freezing point, the water passes in a moment from the utmost liquidity to perfect hardness.

Such an event, therefore, may be denominated *extraordinary*, and requires a pretty strong testimony, to render it credible to people in a warm climate: But still it is not *miraculous*, nor contrary to uniform experience of the course of nature in cases where all the circumstances are the same. The inhabitants of Sumatra have always seen water fluid in their own climate, and the freezing of their rivers ought to be deemed a prodigy: But they never saw water in Muscovy during the winter; and therefore they cannot reasonably be positive what would there be the consequence.[6]

But in order to increase the probability against the testimony of witnesses, let us suppose, that the fact, which they affirm, instead of being only marvellous, is really miraculous; and suppose also, that the testimony considered apart and in itself, amounts to an entire proof; in that case, there is proof against proof, of which the strongest must prevail, but still with a diminution of its force, in proportion to that of its antagonist.

A miracle is a violation of the laws of nature; and as a firm and unalterable experience has established these laws, the proof against a miracle, from the very nature of the fact, is as entire as any argument from experience can possibly be imagined. Why is it more than probable, that all men must die; that lead cannot, of itself, remain suspended in the air; that fire consumes wood, and is extinguished by water; unless it be, that these events are found agreeable to the laws of nature, and there is required a violation of these laws, or in other words, a miracle to prevent them? Nothing is esteemed a miracle, if it ever happen in the common course of nature. It is no miracle that a man, seemingly in good health, should die on a sudden: because such a kind of death, though more unusual than any other, has yet been frequently observed to happen. But it is a miracle, that a dead man should come to life; because that has never been observed in any age or country. There must, therefore, be a uniform experience against every miraculous event, otherwise the event would not merit that appellation. And as a uniform experience amounts to a proof, there is here a direct and full *proof*, from the nature of the fact, against the existence of any miracle; nor can such a proof be destroyed, or the miracle rendered credible, but by an opposite proof, which is superior.

Sometimes an event may not, *in itself, seem* to be contrary to the laws of nature, and yet, if it were real, it might, by reason of some circumstances, be denominated a miracle; because, in *fact*, it is contrary to these laws. Thus if a person claiming a divine authority should command a sick person to be well, a healthful man to fall down dead, the clouds to pour rain, the winds to blow—in short, should order many natural events, which immediately follow upon his command—these might justly be esteemed miracles, because they are really, in this case, contrary to the laws of nature. For if any suspicion remain that the event and command concurred by accident, there is no miracle and no transgression of the laws of nature. If this suspicion be removed, there is evidently a miracle, and a transgression of these laws; because nothing can be more contrary to nature than that the voice or command of a man should have such an influence. A miracle may be accurately defined, *a transgression of a law of nature by a particular volition of the Deity, or by the interposition of some invisible agent.* A miracle may either be discovered by men or not. This alters not its nature and essence. The raising of a house or ship into the air is a visible miracle. The raising of a feather, when the wind wants ever so little of a force requisite for that purpose, is as real a miracle, though not so sensible with regard to us.[7]

The plain consequence is (and it is a general maxim worthy of our attention), 'That no testimony is sufficient to establish a miracle, unless the testimony be of such a kind, that its falsehood would be more miraculous, than the fact, which it endeavours to establish; and even in that case there is a mutual destruction of arguments, and the superior only gives us an assurance suitable to that degree of force, which remains, after deducting the inferior.' When anyone tells me, that he saw a dead man restored to life, I immediately consider with myself, whether it be more probable, that this person should either deceive or be deceived, or that the fact, which he relates, should really have happened. I weigh the one miracle against the other; and according to the superiority, which I discover, I pronounce my decision, and always reject the greater miracle. If the falsehood of his testimony would be more miraculous, than the event which he relates; then, and not till then, can he pretend to command my belief or opinion.

Part 2.

In the foregoing reasoning we have supposed, that the testimony, upon which a miracle is founded, may possibly amount to an entire proof, and that the falsehood of that testimony would be a real prodigy: But it is easy to shew, that we have been a great deal too liberal in our concession, and that there never was a miraculous event established on so full an evidence.

For *first*, there is not to be found, in all history, any miracle attested by a sufficient number of men, of such unquestioned good-sense, education, and learning, as to secure us against all delusion in themselves; of such undoubted integrity, as to place them beyond all suspicion of any design to deceive others; of such credit and reputation in the eyes of mankind, as to have a great deal to lose in case of their being detected in any falsehood; and at the same time, attesting facts performed in such a public manner and in so celebrated a part of the world, as to render the detection unavoidable: All which circumstances are requisite to give us a full assurance in the testimony of men.

Secondly. We may observe in human nature a principle which, if strictly examined, will be found to diminish extremely the assurance, which we might, from human testimony, have, in any kind of prodigy. The maxim, by which we commonly conduct ourselves in our reasonings, is, that the objects, of which we have no experience, resemble those, of which we have; that what we have found to be most usual is always most probable; and that where there is an opposition of arguments, we ought to give the preference to such as are founded on the greatest number of past observations. But though, in proceeding by this rule, we readily reject any fact which is unusual and incredible in an ordinary degree; yet in advancing farther, the mind observes not always the same rule; but when anything is affirmed utterly absurd and miraculous, it rather the more readily admits of such a fact, upon account of that very circumstance, which ought to destroy all its authority. The passion of *surprise* and *wonder*, arising from miracles, being an agreeable emotion, gives a sensible tendency towards the belief of those events, from which it is derived. And this goes so far, that even those who cannot enjoy this pleasure immediately, nor can believe those miraculous events, of which they are informed, yet love to partake of the satisfaction at second-hand or by rebound, and place a pride and delight in exciting the admiration of others.

With what greediness are the miraculous accounts of travellers received, their descriptions of sea and land monsters, their relations of wonderful adventures, strange men, and uncouth manners?

But if the spirit of religion join itself to the love of wonder, there is an end of common sense; and human testimony, in these circumstances, loses all pretensions to authority. A religionist may be an enthusiast,[8] and imagine he sees what has no reality: he may know his narrative to be false, and yet persevere in it, with the best intentions in the world, for the sake of promoting so holy a cause: or even where this delusion has not place, vanity, excited by so strong a temptation, operates on him more powerfully than on the rest of mankind in any other circumstances; and self-interest with equal force. His auditors may not have, and commonly have not, sufficient judgement to canvass his evidence: what judgement they have, they renounce by principle, in these sublime and mysterious subjects: or if they were ever so willing to employ it, passion and a heated imagination disturb the regularity of its operations. Their credulity increases his impudence: and his impudence overpowers their credulity.

Eloquence, when at its highest pitch, leaves little room for reason or reflection; but addressing itself entirely to the fancy or the affections, captivates the willing hearers, and subdues their understanding. Happily, this pitch it seldom attains. But what a Tully or a Demosthenes could scarcely effect over a Roman or Athenian audience, every *Capuchin*, every itinerant or stationary teacher can perform over the generality of mankind, and in a higher degree, by touching such gross and vulgar passions.[9]

The many instances of forged miracles, and prophecies, and supernatural events, which, in all ages, have either been detected by contrary evidence, or which detect themselves by their absurdity, prove sufficiently the strong propensity of mankind to the extraordinary and the marvellous, and ought reasonably to beget a suspicion against all relations of this kind. This is our natural way of thinking, even with regard to the most common and most credible events. For instance: There is no kind of report which rises so easily, and spreads so quickly, especially in country places and provincial towns, as those concerning marriages; insomuch that two young persons of equal condition never see each other twice, but the whole neighbourhood immediately join them together. The pleasure of telling a piece of news so interesting, of propagating it, and of being the first reporters of it, spreads the intelligence. And this is so well known, that no man of sense gives attention to these reports, till he find them confirmed by some greater evidence. Do not the same passions, and others still stronger, incline the generality of mankind to believe and report, with the greatest vehemence and assurance, all religious miracles?

Thirdly. It forms a strong presumption against all supernatural and miraculous relations, that they are observed chiefly to abound among ignorant and barbarous nations; or if a civilized people has ever given admission to any of them, that people will be found to have received them from ignorant and barbarous ancestors, who transmitted them with that inviolable sanction and authority, which always attend received opinions. When we peruse the first histories of all nations, we are apt to imagine ourselves transported into some new world; where the whole frame of nature is disjointed, and every element performs its operations in a different manner, from what it does at present. Battles, revolutions, pestilence, famine and death, are never the effect of those natural causes, which we experience. Prodigies, omens, oracles, judgements, quite obscure the few natural events, that are intermingled with them. But as the former grow thinner every page, in proportion as we advance nearer the enlightened ages, we soon learn, that there is nothing mysterious or supernatural in the case, but that all proceeds from the usual propensity of mankind towards the marvellous, and that, though this inclination may at intervals receive a check from sense and learning, it can never be thoroughly extirpated from human nature.

It is strange, a judicious reader is apt to say, upon the perusal of these wonderful historians, *that such prodigious events never happen in our days*. But it is nothing strange, I hope, that men should lie in all ages. You must surely have seen instances enough of that frailty. You have yourself heard many such marvellous relations started, which, being treated with scorn by all the wise and judicious, have at last been abandoned even by the vulgar. Be assured, that those renowned lies, which have spread and flourished to such a monstrous height, arose from like beginnings; but being sown in a more proper soil, shot up at last into prodigies almost equal to those which they relate.

It was a wise policy in that false prophet, Alexander, who though now forgotten, was once so famous, to lay the first scene of his impostures in Paphlagonia, where, as Lucian tells us, the people were extremely ignorant and stupid, and ready to swallow even the grossest delusion.[10] People at a

distance, who are weak enough to think the matter
at all worth enquiry, have no opportunity of
receiving better information. The stories come
magnified to them by a hundred circumstances.
Fools are industrious in propagating the imposture;
while the wise and learned are contented, in
general, to deride its absurdity, without informing
themselves of the particular facts, by which it may
be distinctly refuted. And thus the impostor above
mentioned was enabled to proceed, from his
ignorant Paphlagonians, to the enlisting of votaries,
even among the Grecian philosophers, and men of
the most eminent rank and distinction in Rome:
nay, could engage the attention of that sage
emperor Marcus Aurelius,[11] so far as to make him
trust the success of a military expedition to his
delusive prophecies.

The advantages are so great, of starting an
imposture among an ignorant people, that, even
though the delusion should be too gross to impose
on the generality of them *(which, though seldom, is
sometimes the case)* it has a much better chance for
succeeding in remote countries, than if the first
scene had been laid in a city renowned for arts and
knowledge. The most ignorant and barbarous of
these barbarians carry the report abroad. None of
their countrymen have a large correspondence, or
sufficient credit and authority to contradict and
beat down the delusion. Men's inclination to the
marvellous has full opportunity to display itself.
And thus a story, which is universally exploded in
the place where it was first started, shall pass for
certain at a thousand miles distance. But had
Alexander fixed his residence at Athens, the
philosophers of that renowned mart of learning had

immediately spread, throughout the whole Roman empire, their sense of the matter; which, being supported by so great authority, and displayed by all the force of reason and eloquence, had entirely opened the eyes of mankind. It is true; Lucian, passing by chance through Paphlagonia, had an opportunity of performing this good office. But, though much to be wished, it does not always happen, that every Alexander meets with a Lucian, ready to expose and detect his impostures.

I may add as a *fourth* reason, which diminishes the authority of prodigies, that there is no testimony for any, even those which have not been expressly detected, that is not opposed by an infinite number of witnesses; so that not only the miracle destroys the credit of testimony, but the testimony destroys itself. To make this the better understood, let us consider, that, in matters of religion, whatever is different is contrary; and that it is impossible the religions of ancient Rome, of Turkey, of Siam, and of China should, all of them, be established on any solid foundation. Every miracle, therefore, pretended to have been wrought in any of these religions (and all of them abound in miracles), as its direct scope is to establish the particular system to which it is attributed; so has it the same force, though more indirectly, to overthrow every other system. In destroying a rival system, it likewise destroys the credit of those miracles, on which that system was established; so that all the prodigies of different religions are to be regarded as contrary facts, and the evidences of these prodigies, whether weak or strong, as opposite to each other. According to this method of reasoning, when we believe any miracle of

Mahomet or his successors,[12] we have for our
warrant the testimony of a few barbarous Arabians:
And on the other hand, we are to regard the
authority of Titus Livius, Plutarch, Tacitus, and, in
short, of all the authors and witnesses, Grecian,
Chinese, and Roman Catholic, who have related
any miracle in their particular religion;[13] I say, we
are to regard their testimony in the same light as if
they had mentioned that Mahometan miracle, and
had in express terms contradicted it, with the same
certainty as they have for the miracle they relate.
This argument may appear over subtile and
refined; but is not in reality different from the
reasoning of a judge, who supposes, that the credit
of two witnesses, maintaining a crime against any
one, is destroyed by the testimony of two others,
who affirm him to have been two hundred leagues
distant, at the same instant when the crime is said
to have been committed.

One of the best attested miracles in all profane
history, is that which Tacitus reports of
Vespasian,[14] who cured a blind man in Alexandria,
by means of his spittle, and a lame man by the
mere touch of his foot; in obedience to a vision of
the god Serapis, who had enjoined them to have
recourse to the Emperor, for these miraculous
cures. The story may be seen in that fine
historian;[15] where every circumstance seems to add
weight to the testimony, and might be displayed at
large with all the force of argument and eloquence,
if any one were now concerned to enforce the
evidence of that exploded and idolatrous
superstition. The gravity, solidity, age, and probity
of so great an emperor, who, through the whole
course of his life, conversed in a familiar manner

with his friends and courtiers, and never affected those extraordinary airs of divinity assumed by Alexander and Demetrius.[16] The historian, a contemporary writer, noted for candour and veracity, and withal, the greatest and most penetrating genius, perhaps, of all antiquity; and so free from any tendency to credulity, that he even lies under the contrary imputation, of atheism and profaneness: The persons, from whose authority he related the miracle, of established character for judgement and veracity, as we may well presume; eye-witnesses of the fact, and confirming their testimony, after the Flavian family was despoiled of the empire[17] and could no longer give any reward, as the price of a lie. *Utrumque, qui interfuere, nunc quoque memorant, postquam nullum mendacio pretium.* [Those who were present still tell the tale now, when there is no longer any reward for lying.] To which if we add the public nature of the facts, as related, it will appear, that no evidence can well be supposed stronger for so gross and so palpable a falsehood.

There is also a memorable story related by Cardinal de Retz,[18] which may well deserve our consideration. When that intriguing politician fled into Spain, to avoid the persecution of his enemies, he passed through Saragossa, the capital of Aragon, where he was shewn, in the cathedral, a man, who had served seven years as a doorkeeper, and was well known to every body in town, that had ever paid his devotions at that church. He had been seen, for so long a time, wanting a leg; but recovered that limb by the rubbing of holy oil upon the stump; and the cardinal assures us that he saw him with two legs. This miracle was vouched by all the canons of the church; and the whole company in town were appealed to for a confirmation of the fact; whom the cardinal found, by their zealous devotion, to be thorough believers of the miracle. Here the relater was also contemporary to the supposed prodigy, of an incredulous and libertine character, as well as of great genius; the miracle of so *singular* a nature as could scarcely admit of a counterfeit, and the witnesses very numerous, and all of them, in a manner, spectators of the fact, to which they gave their testimony. And what adds mightily to the force of the evidence, and may double our surprise on this occasion, is, that the cardinal himself, who relates the story, seems not to give any credit to it, and consequently cannot be suspected of any concurrence in the holy fraud. He considered justly, that it was not requisite, in order to reject a fact of this nature, to be able accurately to disprove the testimony, and to trace its falsehood, through all the circumstances of knavery and credulity which produced it. He knew, that, as this was commonly altogether impossible at any small distance of time and place; so was it extremely difficult, even where one was immediately present, by reason of the bigotry, ignorance, cunning, and roguery of a great part of mankind. He therefore concluded, like a just reasoner, that such an evidence carried falsehood upon the very face of it, and that a miracle, supported by any human testimony, was more properly a subject of derision than of argument.

There surely never was a greater number of miracles ascribed to one person, than those, which were lately said to have been wrought in France upon the tomb of Abbé Paris,[19] the famous

Jansenist, with whose sanctity the people were so long deluded. The curing of the sick, giving hearing to the deaf, and sight to the blind, were every where talked of as the usual effects of that holy sepulchre. But what is more extraordinary; many of the miracles were immediately proved upon the spot, before judges of unquestioned integrity, attested by witnesses of credit and distinction, in a learned age, and on the most eminent theatre that is now in the world. Nor is this all: a relation of them was published and dispersed everywhere; nor were the *Jesuits*, though a learned body, supported by the civil magistrate, and determined enemies to those opinions, in whose favour the miracles were said to have been wrought, ever able distinctly to refute or detect them.[20] Where shall we find such a number of circumstances, agreeing to the corroboration of one fact? And what have we to oppose to such a cloud of witnesses, but the absolute impossibility or miraculous nature of the events, which they relate? And this surely, in the eyes of all reasonable people, will alone be regarded as a sufficient refutation.

This book was writ by Mons. Montgeron, counsellor or judge of the parliament of Paris, a man of figure and character, who was also a martyr to the cause, and is now said to be somewhere in a dungeon on account of his book.

There is another book in three volumes (called *Recueil des Miracles de l'Abbé Paris*) giving an account of many of these miracles, and accompanied with prefatory discourses, which are very well written. There runs, however, through the whole of these a ridiculous comparison between the miracles of our Saviour and those of the Abbé;

wherein it is asserted, that the evidence for the latter is equal to that for the former: As if the testimony of men could ever be put in the balance with that of God himself, who conducted the pen of the inspired writers. If these writers, indeed, were to be considered merely as human testimony, the French author is very moderate in his comparison; since he might, with some appearance of reason, pretend, that the Jansenist miracles much surpass the other in evidence and authority.[21] The following circumstances are drawn from authentic papers, inserted in the above-mentioned book.

Many of the miracles of Abbé Paris were proved immediately by witnesses before the officiality or bishop's court at Paris, under the eye of cardinal Noailles, whose character for integrity and capacity was never contested even by his enemies.

His successor in the archbishopric was an enemy to the Jansenists, and for that reason promoted to the see by the court. Yet 22 rectors or *curés* of Paris, with infinite earnestness, press him to examine those miracles, which they assert to be known to the whole world, and undisputably certain: But he wisely forbore.

The Molinist party had tried to discredit these miracles in one instance, that of Mademoiselle le Franc. But, besides that their proceedings were in many respects the most irregular in the world, particularly in citing only a few of the Jansenist witnesses, whom they tampered with: Besides this, I say, they soon found themselves overwhelmed by a cloud of new witnesses, one hundred and twenty in number, most of them persons of credit and substance in Paris, who gave oath for the miracle. This was accompanied with a solemn and earnest appeal to the parliament. But the parliament were forbidden by authority to meddle in the affair. It was at last observed, that where men are heated by zeal and enthusiasm, there is no degree of human testimony so strong as may not be procured for the greatest absurdity: And those who will be so silly as to examine the affair by that medium, and seek particular flaws in the testimony, are almost sure to be confounded. It must be a miserable imposture, indeed, that does not prevail in that contest.

All who have been in France about that time have heard of the reputation of Mons. Heraut, the *lieutenant de Police*, whose vigilance, penetration, activity, and extensive intelligence have been much talked of. This magistrate, who by the nature of his office is almost absolute, was invested with full powers, on purpose to suppress or discredit these miracles; and he frequently seized immediately, and examined the witnesses and subjects of them: But never could reach any thing satisfactory against them.

In the case of Mademoiselle Thibaut he sent the famous De Sylva to examine her; whose evidence is very curious. The physician declares, that it was impossible she could have been so ill as was proved by witnesses; because it was impossible she could, in so short a time, have recovered so perfectly as he found her. He reasoned, like a man of sense, from natural causes; but the opposite party told him, that the whole was a miracle, and that his evidence was the very best proof of it.

The Molinists were in a sad dilemma. They durst not assert the absolute insufficiency of human evidence, to prove a miracle. They were obliged to say, that these miracles were wrought by witchcraft and the devil. But they were told, that this was the resource of the Jews of old.

No Jansenist was ever embarrassed to account for the cessation of the miracles, when the church-yard was shut up by the king's edict. It was the touch of the tomb, which produced these extraordinary effects; and when no one could approach the tomb, no effects could be expected. God, indeed, could have thrown down the walls in a moment; but he is master of his own graces and works, and it belongs not to us to account for them. He did not throw down the walls of every city like those of Jericho, on the sounding of the rams horns, nor break up the prison of every apostle, like that of St. Paul.

No less a man, than the Duc de Chatillon, a duke and peer of France, of the highest rank and family, gives evidence of a miraculous cure, performed upon a servant of his, who had lived several years in his house with a visible and palpable infirmity.

I shall conclude with observing, that no clergy are more celebrated for strictness of life and manners than the secular clergy of France, particularly the rectors or curés of Paris, who bear testimony to these impostures.

The learning, genius, and probity of the gentlemen, and the austerity of the nuns of Port-Royal, have been much celebrated all over Europe. Yet they all give evidence for a miracle, wrought on the niece of the famous Pascal, whose sanctity of life, as well as extraordinary capacity, is well known. The famous Racine gives an account of this miracle in his famous history of Port-Royal, and fortifies it with all the proofs, which a multitude of nuns, priests, physicians, and men of the world, all of them of undoubted credit, could bestow upon it. Several men of letters, particularly the bishop of Tournay, thought this miracle so certain, as to employ it in the refutation of atheists and freethinkers. The queen-regent of France, who was extremely prejudiced against the Port-Royal, sent her own physician to examine the miracle, who returned an absolute convert. In short, the supernatural cure was so uncontestable, that it saved, for a time, that famous monastery from the ruin with which it was threatened by the Jesuits. Had it been a cheat, it had certainly been detected by such sagacious and powerful antagonists, and must have hastened the ruin of the contrivers. Our divines, who can build up a formidable castle from such despicable materials; what a prodigious fabric could they have reared from these and many other circumstances, which I have not mentioned! How often would the great names of Pascal, Racine, Arnaud, Nicole, have resounded in our ears? But if they be wise, they had better adopt the miracle, as being more worth, a thousand times, than all the rest of their collection. Besides, it may serve very much to their purpose. For that miracle was really performed by the touch of an authentic holy prickle of the holy thorn, which composed the holy crown, which, &c.

Is the consequence just, because some human testimony has the utmost force and authority in some cases, when it relates the battle of Philippi or Pharsalia for instance;[22] that therefore all kinds of testimony must, in all cases, have equal force and authority? Suppose that the Caesarean and

Pompeian factions had, each of them, claimed the victory in these battles, and that the historians of each party had uniformly ascribed the advantage to their own side; how could mankind, at this distance, have been able to determine between them? The contrariety is equally strong between the miracles related by Herodotus or Plutarch, and those delivered by Mariana, Bede, or any monkish historian.[23]

The wise lend a very academic faith to every report which favours the passion of the reporter; whether it magnifies his country, his family, or himself, or in any other way strikes in with his natural inclinations and propensities. But what greater temptation than to appear a missionary, a prophet, an ambassador from heaven? Who would not encounter many dangers and difficulties, in order to attain so sublime a character? Or if, by the help of vanity and a heated imagination, a man has first made a convert of himself, and entered seriously into the delusion; who ever scruples to make use of pious frauds, in support of so holy and meritorious a cause?

The smallest spark may here kindle into the greatest flame; because the materials are always prepared for it. The *avidum genus auricularum*,[24] the gazing populace, receive greedily, without examination, whatever soothes superstition, and promotes wonder.

How many stories of this nature have, in all ages, been detected and exploded in their infancy? How many more have been celebrated for a time, and have afterwards sunk into neglect and oblivion? Where such reports, therefore, fly about, the solution of the phenomenon is obvious; and we judge in conformity to regular experience and observation, when we account for it by the known and natural principles of credulity and delusion. And shall we, rather than have a recourse to so natural a solution, allow of a miraculous violation of the most established laws of nature?

I need not mention the difficulty of detecting a falsehood in any private or even public history, at the place, where it is said to happen; much more when the scene is removed to ever so small a distance. Even a court of judicature, with all the authority, accuracy, and judgement, which they can employ, find themselves often at a loss to distinguish between truth and falsehood in the most recent actions. But the matter never comes to any issue, if trusted to the common method of altercation and debate and flying rumours; especially when men's passions have taken part on either side.

In the infancy of new religions, the wise and learned commonly esteem the matter too inconsiderable to deserve their attention or regard. And when afterwards they would willingly detect the cheat, in order to undeceive the deluded multitude, the season is now past, and the records and witnesses, which might clear up the matter, have perished beyond recovery.

No means of detection remain, but those which must be drawn from the very testimony itself of the reporters: and these, though always sufficient with the judicious and knowing, are commonly too fine to fall under the comprehension of the vulgar.

Upon the whole, then, it appears, that no testimony for any kind of miracle has ever amounted to a probability, much less to a proof;

and that, even supposing it amounted to a proof, it would be opposed by another proof; derived from the very nature of the fact, which it would endeavour to establish. It is experience only, which gives authority to human testimony; and it is the same experience, which assures us of the laws of nature. When, therefore, these two kinds of experience are contrary, we have nothing to do but subtract the one from the other, and embrace an opinion, either on one side or the other, with that assurance which arises from the remainder. But according to the principle here explained, this substraction, with regard to all popular religions, amounts to an entire annihilation; and therefore we may establish it as a maxim, that no human testimony can have such force as to prove a miracle, and make it a just foundation for any such system of religion.

I beg the limitations here made may be remarked, when I say, that a miracle can never be proved, so as to be the foundation of a system of religion. For I own, that otherwise, there may possibly be miracles, or violations of the usual course of nature, of such a kind as to admit of proof from human testimony; though, perhaps, it wil be impossible to find any such in all the records of history. Thus, suppose, all authors, in all languages, agree, that, from the first of January 1600, there was a total darkness over the whole earth for eight days: suppose that the tradition of this extraordinary event is still strong and lively among the people: that all travellers, who return from foreign countries, bring us accounts of the same tradition, without the least variation or contradiction: it is evident, that our present philosophers, instead of doubting the fact, ought to receive it as certain, and ought to search for the causes whence it might be derived. The decay, corruption, and dissolution of nature, is an event rendered probable by so many analogies, that any phenomenon, which seems to have a tendency towards that catastrophe, comes within the reach of human testimony, if that testimony be very extensive and uniform.

But suppose, that all the historians who treat of England, should agree, that, on the first of January 1600, Queen Elizabeth died; that both before and after her death she was seen by her physicians and the whole court, as is usual with persons of her rank; that her successor was acknowledged and proclaimed by the parliament; and that, after being interred a month, she again appeared, resumed the throne, and governed England for three years: I must confess that I should be surprised at the concurrence of so many odd circumstances, but should not have the least inclination to believe so miraculous an event. I should not doubt of her pretended death, and of those other public circumstances that followed it: I should only assert it to have been pretended, and that it neither was, nor possibly could be real. You would in vain object to me the difficulty, and almost impossibility of deceiving the world in an affair of such consequence; the wisdom and solid judgement of that renowned queen; with the little or no advantage which she could reap from so poor an artifice: All this might astonish me; but I would still reply, that the knavery and folly of men are such common phenomena, that I should rather believe the most extraordinary events to arise from their concurrence, than admit of so signal a violation of the laws of nature.

But should this miracle be ascribed to any new system of religion; men, in all ages, have been so much imposed on by ridiculous stories of that kind, that this very circumstance would be a full proof of a cheat, and sufficient, with all men of sense, not only to make them reject the fact, but even reject it without farther examination. Though the Being to whom the miracle is ascribed, be, in this case, Almighty, it does not, upon that account, become a whit more probable; since it is impossible for us to know the attributes or actions of such a Being, otherwise than from the experience which we have of his productions, in the usual course of nature. This still reduces us to past observation, and obliges us to compare the instances of the violation of truth in the testimony of men, with those of the violation of the laws of nature by miracles, in order to judge which of them is most likely and probable. As the violations of truth are more common in the testimony concerning religious miracles, than in that concerning any other matter of fact; this must diminish very much the authority of the former testimony, and make us form a general resolution, never to lend any attention to it, with whatever specious pretence it may be covered.

Lord Bacon seems to have embraced the same principles of reasonings.[25] 'We ought,' says he, 'to make a collection or particular history of all monsters and prodigious births or productions, and in a word of every thing new, rare, and extraordinary in nature. But this must be done with the most severe scrutiny, lest we depart from truth. Above all, every relation must be considered as suspicious, which depends in any degree upon religion, as the prodigies of Livy: And no less so, every thing that is to be found in the writers of natural magic or alchimy, or such authors, who seem, all of them, to have an unconquerable appetite for falsehood and fable.'

I am the better pleased with the method of reasoning here delivered, as I think it may serve to confound those dangerous friends or disguised enemies to the *Christian Religion*, who have undertaken to defend it by the principles of human reason. Our most holy religion is founded on *Faith*, not on reason; and it is a sure method of exposing it to put it to such a trial as it is, by no means, fitted to endure. To make this more evident, let us examine those miracles, related in scripture; and not to lose ourselves in too wide a field, let us confine ourselves to such as we find in the *Pentateuch*,[26] which we shall examine, according to the principles of these pretended Christians, not as the word or testimony of God himself, but as the production of a mere human writer and historian. Here then we are first to consider a book, presented to us by a barbarous and ignorant people, written in an age when they were still more barbarous, and in all probability long after the facts which it relates, corroborated by no concurring testimony, and resembling those fabulous accounts, which every nation gives of its origin. Upon reading this book, we find it full of prodigies and miracles. It gives an account of a state of the world and of human nature entirely different from the present: Of our fall from that state: Of the age of man, extended to near a thousand years: Of the destruction of the world by a deluge: Of the arbitrary choice of one people, as the favourites of heaven; and that people the countrymen of the author: Of their deliverance from bondage by prodigies the most astonishing imaginable: I desire any one to lay his hand upon his heart, and after a serious consideration declare, whether he thinks that the falsehood of such a book, supported by such a testimony, would be more extraordinary and miraculous than all the miracles it relates; which is, however, necessary to make it be received, according to the measures of probability above established.

What we have said of miracles may be applied, without any variation, to prophecies; and indeed, all prophecies are real miracles, and as such only, can be admitted as proofs of any revelation. If it did not exceed the capacity of human nature to foretell future events, it would be absurd to employ any prophecy as an argument for a divine mission or authority from heaven. So that, upon the whole, we may conclude, that the *Christian Religion* not only was at first attended with miracles, but even at this day cannot be believed by any reasonable person without one. Mere reason is insufficient to convince us of its veracity: And whoever is moved by *Faith* to assent to it, is conscious of a continued miracle in his own person, which subverts all the principles of his understanding, and gives him a determination to believe what is most contrary to custom and experience.[27]

Notes

1. John Tillotson (1630–94) was an influential Presbyterian clergyman who in 1662 submitted to the Act of Uniformity. In 1691 he was appointed Archbishop of Canterbury. Reference works tell us, tactfully, that "in later years his sermons emphasized the practical ... rather than the theological aspects of Christianity".

Certainly the fact that he appears to have believed that the doctrine of the Real Presence, as construed by Roman Catholics, actually contradicts sensory experience, suggests a remarkable lack of theological sophistication. For the peculiarly Roman Catholic doctrine of Transubstantiation, explaining how it is supposed to be possible to be really present though wholly unobservable, is a doctrine maintaining that, in a properly conducted Mass, the substance of the bread and the substance of the wine are transformed into the substance of the body and the substance of the blood of the Christ, *all the sensory appearances remaining the same.*

2. 'Moral evidence' here means evidence from and about matters of fact. The contrast is with matters which can be demonstrated as deducible from logically necessary truths. It is the same use of the word 'moral' as in the fossil phrase 'moral certainty'.

3. Here and subsequently Hume should have written not 'experiments' but 'experiences'.

4. Cato the Younger (95–46 B.C.), a Roman politician and

Of Miracles

moralist, described as "a philosophical patriot" because of his
adhesion to the Stoic philosophy.

5. The reference here is to John Locke *An Essay Concerning
Human Understanding*, III (vi) 13 and IV (xvi) 5–6. The "first
relations" are the first stories related.

6. In Hume's original, this paragraph was a footnote.

7. This paragraph was originally printed as a footnote.

8. An enthusiast in the eighteenth century was a fanatic.
So the epigraphic tributes in English churches to divines who
were "religious but without enthusiasm" lacked for
contemporaries the piquant flavour which they have for us
today!

9. Tully was Marcus Tullius Cicero (106–43 B.C.), a Roman
politician and orator. His various, wholly derivative
philosophical work, mainly written in the last few months
before his political murder, were extremely influential in
Hume's day; partly because the sources from which they were
derived have been largely lost. Demosthenes (384–322 B.C.)
was an Athenian politician and orator. A Capuchin is a Friar of
one branch of the order of St. Francis.

10. Lucian, in the second century A.D., was a Greek
satirical writer. His *Alexander, or the False Prophet* was an
account of the faking of a manifestation of Asclepius,
(Aesculapius) a god of healing, in the form of a serpent with a
human head. Paphlagonia was a territory in the north of what
is now Asiatic Turkey.

11. Marcus Aurelius (121–80 A.D.) was at this time the
Roman Emperor, and thus the supreme ruler over
Paphlagonia. He was an adherent of the Stoic philosophy, and
author of the classic *Meditations.*

12. 'Mahomet' was the older spelling of Mohammed
(c.570–632 A.D.), the Prophet of Islam.

13. Titus Livius (59 B.C.–17 A.D.) was a Roman historian
of Rome, more usually referred to as Livy. Plutarch (c.46–c.120
A.D.) was a Greek writer of biographies—the 'parallel lives'.
Hume refers to his *Life of Cato* in a note to the mention in Part
I, above. Tacitus (c.57 A.D.–c.120 A.D.) was a notably sceptical
and astringent Roman historian of Imperial Rome.

14. Vespasian (9–79 A.D.) was a tough and successful
soldier who became a Roman Emperor. Fully to appreciate this
story you need to recognize that Vespasian and his soldiers,

whether rightly or wrongly, amply had the same contempt for Egyptians as was common in the British Eighth Army during World War II.

15. Hume here refers us to Tacitus *Histories* V 8, and this reference has been reprinted in every successive edition of the *First Inquiry* from 1777 until Peter Nidditch's 1975 revision of L. A. Selby-Bigge's long standard Clarendon Press version. It would seem that—notwithstanding all the controversy which there has been about this Section X 'Of Miracles'—no one ever looked the passage up in Tacitus until I did this in preparing my *Hume's Philosophy of Belief* (London: Routledge and Kegan Paul, 1961). I then discovered that 'V 8' should have been 'IV 81'. Several morals may be drawn from this remarkable fact.

Hume also notes that the inferior authority Suetonius (c.69–c.140 A.D.) gives a similar account in his life of Vespasian.

16. Alexander the Great (356–323 B.C.) and Demetrius I of Macedonia (336–283 B.C.).

17. The Flavian Emperors were Vespasian and his sons Titus (c.40–81 A.D.) and Domitian (51–96 A.D.)

18. Cardinal de Retz (1614–79) was an Archbishop of Paris, author of *Mémoires*.

19. François de Paris (1690–1727) was a follower of Cornelius Jansen (1585–1638), a Bishop of Ypres in Flanders. Jansenism was a doctrine of moral austerity and of the dependence of all virtue on divine grace, a doctrine expounded most notably in Jansen's 1640 *Augustinus*. It was adopted by the Cistercian Convent of Port-Royal, with which the mathematician and philosopher Blaise Pascal (1623–62) and other leading French intellectuals were closely associated. Among these Arnauld and Nicole produced in 1662 *L'Art du Penser*, a very influential work usually known as the *Port-Royal Logic*.

As Hume proceeds to make clear, the question of the genuineness of the miracles supposedly occurring "upon the tomb of Abbé Paris" was crucial for both the Jansenists and their Jesuit opponents. For they were agreed that the ocurrence of any genuine miracles must constitute decisive Divine endorsement for the doctrinal claims of the party thus favoured.

20. At this point in Hume's original came the reference to

a gleeful footnote, 12 paragraphs long, giving more details of the miracles allegedly wrought on and around the tomb of the Abbé Paris. The footnote, commencing "This book was writ by Mons. Montgeron", is here incorporated into the text.

21. Many readers, including too many of those paid to know better, have, both here and elsewhere, failed to recognize Hume's irony. It may, therefore, be necessary to indicate that, of course, he himself regarded this comparison not as ridiculous but rather as totally to the point and absolutely devastating.

22. Philippi was a city in Macedonia where in 42 B.C. the army of Octavian, the future first Roman Emperor Augustus, and Mark Antony, defeated the republican army: see, for instance, Shakespeare's *Julius Caesar*. Pharsalia was a city in Thessaly, a part of what is now Northern Greece, near where in 48 B.C. Caesar's army defeated that of Pompey.

23. Herodotus of Halicarnassus in Asia Minor was a Greek historian working in the fifth century B.C. Generally allowed to be 'the father of history' Herodotus normally dissociates himself from whatever tales of the seemingly miraculous he feels bound to record. Juan Mariana (1536–1623 A.D.) was a Spanish Jesuit who wrote Spanish history. St. Bede (c.673–735 A.D.) is often called, perhaps too flatteringly, 'the father of Engish history.'

24. This phrase ['race eager for hearsay'] is taken from the secularizing Roman poet Lucretius *(de Rerum Natura* [On the Nature of Things] IV 594).

25. Francis Bacon (1561–1626) under James I, and until his disgrace in an earlier Water Gate affair, was Lord Chancellor of England. Bacon is usually rated the first in the long line of British empiricist philosophers. The passage quoted is Aphorism 29 of Book II of his *Novum Organum*, a work in which he tried to improve upon previous conceptions of scientific method.

26. 'Pentateuch' is a term for the first five books of the *Old Testament* (Genesis, Exodus, Leviticus, Numbers, and Deuteronomy.)

27. This final paragraph has been seen as more scandalous than any other passage in all Hume's writings. Fully to understand and to savour it we need to know what was, in his day, the regular teaching of all the Reformed Churches. Faith,

it was held, or even a correct reading of the Scriptures, is impossible save to those vouch-safed Divine Grace; a Grace miraculously, and it would seem arbitrarily, conferred upon all but only the Elect.

THE VICE-CONSUL

THE VICE-

Marguerite Duras

CONSUL

A · PANTHEON · MODERN · WRITERS · ORIGINAL

Translated from the French
By Eileen Ellenbogen

PANTHEON · BOOKS · NEW · YORK

FOR JEAN C.

Library of Congress Cataloging-in-Publication Data

Duras, Marguerite.
The vice-consul.
(A Pantheon modern writers original)
Translation of: Le vice-consul.
I. Title.   II. Series.
PQ2607.U8245V4713   1987   843'.912   86-43092
ISBN 0-394-55898-7
ISBN 0-394-75026-8 (pbk.)

First American Edition

Manufactured in the United States of America

She walks on, writes Peter Morgan.

How to avoid going back? Get lost. I don't know how. You'll learn. I need some signpost to lead me astray. Make your mind a blank. Refuse to recognize familiar landmarks. Turn your steps towards the most hostile point on the horizon, towards the vast marshlands, bewilderingly criss-crossed by a thousand causeways.

She does so. Day after day she walks, at times following the causeways, at others splashing through water. Reaching the limit of one complex of marshes, she goes on to the next, and the next.

She is still on the plain of Tonle Sap, still in familiar territory.

She has yet to learn that the distant point on the horizon towards which her steps are directed is not necessarily the most hostile of places, though it may seem so. Hostility is most likely to be found where it is least expected.

With bowed head, she reaches the most hostile point on the horizon. With bowed head, she sees the mud littered with shells which she recognizes. They are the shells of Tonle Sap.

Only put your mind to it, and what repels you today will appeal to you tomorrow. That is what she thinks she heard her mother say, before she drove her out. She believes it to be true. She persists, she walks, she despairs: I'm too young, I must go back. 'If you come back,' her mother said, 'I shall poison your rice. I will kill you.'

I

With bowed head, she walks. She walks. Her strength is very great. Her hunger is as great as her strength. She walks in circles in the flat countryside of Tonle Sap, where sky meets earth edge-to-edge, in a straight line. She achieves nothing. She stops, moves on, moves on, with the sky like an inverted bowl overhead.

Her hunger and determination are trampled into the soil of Tonle Sap. They proliferate. They spread. Footprints, scattered like seed over the land, put forth shoots. She has lost all sense of direction. In her sleep, she sees her mother standing over her, brandishing a cane: 'Tomorrow, at sunrise, you must go. You, my child, being with child, are old. You have no husband. You will grow old alone. My duty is to the younger ones who, in their turn, will also leave us. Go. Go far. You must never come back. Never. Go very far, so far that it will be impossible for me even to imagine the place where you are. Pay your respects. Prostrate yourself before your mother, and go.'

Her father said: 'If I am not mistaken, there is a kinsman of ours in the Plain of Birds. He has few children. He might take you in as a servant.' She has not yet begun to ask the way. It rains every day. The sky is in perpetual turmoil, with clouds scudding towards the north. The great lake is swollen. Wind fills the sails of junks on the lake of Tonle Sap. The opposite shore of the lake is visible only when the sky clears between storms. Seeming to rise out of the water, a row of bluish palm trees is silhouetted against the sky.

At the start, she had an uninterrupted view across the lake. She has never been to the other side. Might not that be the place where she could begin to lose herself? No, from there she would be able to see across to the shore on this side, her birthplace. The waters of Tonle Sap are stagnant, muddy. No ripple breaks their surface. They breed fear.

She can no longer see the lake. She has come to another

vast stretch of alien, deserted marshland, criss-crossed by causeways. At present, there is not a living thing in sight. Everything is still. She reaches the far side of the vast complex of marshes, which stretches behind her like a dazzling sheet of metal, until it is blotted out by rain. She sees people and animals move across it.

Then, one morning, she comes to a river. There is promise in the gentle, drowsy flow of its waters. No one, her father once told her, following the course of the Tonle Sap, need ever despair. Its silt nourished fertile banks, in and out of season. The lake was a fresh-water sea, he said, and if there were any children left alive in this region, it was thanks to the abundance of fish in the waters of Tonle Sap. She walks. Having stumbled upon the river, she follows it upstream for three days. She reckons that when she comes to the end of it, she will have reached the north, the northern shore of the lake. There she will stop, looking out across the lake. There she will stay. At each stopping place, she examines her large feet, with their toughened soles, like tire-treads, and rubs them. She finds food: wild rice, mangoes and bunches of bananas. For six days, she walks.

She stops. Surely she has not walked as far, since she turned north and began following the river, as she had before she came to it? She walks on, keeping close to the river, following its twists and turns. Sometimes, at night, she swims. She sets off again. She looks about her: surely, the buffalo on the other side of the river are stockier than any she has seen before? She stops. The child in her womb is growing more and more active. It is as though fish were snapping in her belly, or the insufferable infant were happily beating a drum.

She asks the way to the Plain of Birds, promising herself that, when she finds out where it lies, she will turn her back on it, and go in the opposite direction. She must try, by

every means, to lose her way: by travelling north, by-passing her own village, taking the road to Thailand, stopping before she gets to Thailand. The river comes to an end in the north. There, I shall break this habit I have got into of keeping close to the water. Before I reach Thailand, I shall find a place, and stay there. To her eyes, the lands of the south melt into the sea. The north is solid.

No one can tell her the way to the Plain of Birds. She walks. The Tonle Sap rises in the north, as do all the tributaries that flow into it. These can be seen, like tresses streaming from the head of a giant whose face is turned towards the south. Climb, until you come to the roots of those flowing tresses, and the whole of the southern region will be spread out at your feet, including your own village. The herds of stocky buffalo, the pinkish rock, lumps of which have fallen into the rice-fields here and there, these and other familiar features do not necessarily mean that she is on the wrong road. The ritual encirclement of her own village is, she believes, at an end. She made a false start. At the beginning, she tells herself, she was a prey to self-deception. Now, I am really leaving home. I have made my choice. I am going north.

She is mistaken. The river she has been following upstream is the Stung Pursat which rises in the Cardamom Hills, in the south. She gazes at the range of mountains ahead, and asks if they are in Thailand. She is told they are not. They are Cambodian mountains. In the middle of the day, she lies down to rest in a banana grove, and falls asleep.

Hunger overwhelms her. The altitude, to which she is not yet acclimatized, does not trouble her much. It merely makes her feel drowsy. Hunger takes a grip on her up here

4

in the foot-hills. She begins to sleep a great deal. She sleeps. She gets up. She walks, generally making for the mountains, as, hitherto, she has made for the north. She sleeps.

She searches for food. She sleeps. She does not go forward as she did when crossing the marshes of Tonle Sap. She wavers. She goes round in circles. She comes to a town which, she is told, is Pursat. She makes a circuit of it, keeping to the outskirts. Pursat is behind her. She follows a zig-zag course which, in the long run, takes her nearer to the mountains. She never asks anyone to point the way to Tonle Sap. If she were to ask that, she would only be told lies. No one, she believes, would be willing to show her the way home.

She comes upon a disused gravel pit. She climbs in and lies down to sleep. It is on the outskirts of Pursat. From the gravel pit, she can see rooftops. At one time, she had the impression that she had been two months away from home, but by now she has lost all sense of time. There are thousands of them hovering on the outskirts of Pursat, women driven out of their homes, old men, cheerful simpletons. They meet, in their search for food, but never exchange a word. Mother Earth, feed me. There is fruit, there is slush, there are stones of many colours. She has not yet learned the trick of catching fish when they are drifting sluggishly, close to river banks. Her mother said: 'Eat. Don't you go grieving for your mother. Eat. Eat.' While others are resting, she searches. She searches for a long time. Mother Earth, give me something to chew. She picks fruit when she can get it, wild bananas, rice-shoots, mangoes. Everything she can find, she takes back to the pit and eats. She chews the young rice, and it slips down, warm and sweetish, like gruel. She sleeps. Rice-shoots, mangoes, how much she depends upon them. She sleeps. She wakes and looks about her. Looking right from inside the gravel pit, she sees the town of Pursat on a hill, and the straight line joining earth and sky, the horizon of

her childhood. Nothing else. She had not realized that teeming life could go on in the midst of great empty spaces. She had not realized that there was so much empty space on the plain of Tonle Sap, until now, seeing it from here. To the left of the gravel pit loom the Cardamom Hills, trees piercing the sky, gaping holes, some pink, some white, in the rockface. The rumble of tracked vehicles can be heard on the mountains where these holes are, as well as the thud of falling rocks, and the shouting of men. How long have these sounds been reverberating round her?

How long since the Cardamoms first loomed up in front of her, behind her? How long had she been in sight of the river, turgid with clay, thick as porridge, after the rain? This river, this other river, which showed her the way to this place.

Her belly is growing more and more distended, until her dress is stretched taut across it. Every day it rides up a little higher, until she has to walk with her knees exposed. Perhaps as an effect of the altitude, the texture of her distended belly remains very fine and delicate. It feels warm and soft, as she lies among the stones. It makes her think of succulent food, in which she longs to sink her teeth. Often it rains. Her hunger is always greater after the rain. The child devours everything, rice-shoots and mangoes. The strangest thing of all is that no amount of food can satisfy her hunger.

She wakes. She goes out and wanders in the fields, as she did on the northern shore of Tonle Sap. Occasionally, she meets someone on the way, and asks them to direct her to the Plain of Birds. Either they do not know or they will not tell her. But she keeps on asking. Each time she draws a blank, the Plain of Birds looms larger, takes a firmer grip on her. But at last she finds an old man who is able to direct her. The Plain of Birds? Follow the Mekong River, that must be the way. But how do I get to the Mekong? Follow the Stung

6

Pursat downstream until you reach Lake Tonle Sap, and when you get there, keep going south. All rivers, everywhere, flow into the sea. The Plain of the Water Birds is not far from the sea. Maybe, but what if one chose to follow the Stung Pursat upstream, where would that lead one? Presumably, one would come up against an impassable barrier of mountains. But what lies behind the mountains? The Gulf of Siam, so it is said. But if I were you, child, I should go south, where God's gifts are said to be found in greater abundance.

Now she knows the direction in which Tonle Sap lies, and where she is in relation to it.

She remains in the gravel pit on the outskirts of Pursat.

She goes out. Occasionally she lingers at the door of some isolated straw hut, but always, before very long, someone comes out and drives her away. At first, she does not venture into the villages. Soon she discovers that wherever she stands, some way off from a lonely hut, or at the end of a village street, someone, sooner or later, will always drive her away. So she hides in the clumps of bamboo that grow beside the river, and awaits her opportunity to pass through the village unnoticed, or at least indistinguishable from all the other beggars threading their way among the stalls at the local markets. The soup vendors walk among them as they stand gaping at the gleaming cuts of pork on the stalls, above which, closer to the meat than they are, hover clouds of bluebottles. From the old market women and the soup vendors, she begs a bowl of rice. She does not always ask for rice, sometimes it is a meat bone or a bit of fish, any old, stale fish. What harm is there in asking for a morsel of stale fish? Because she is so very young, the occasional stall-holder takes pity on her and gives her something, but, more often than not, the answer is no. No, because if I do, you'll be back tomorrow, and the next day, and the next. They look her straight in the face: no.

In the gravel pit, on the ground, she finds strands of hair, her hair. She pulls her hair and it comes out in handfuls. She feels no pain. It is only hair. Pain is always in front, in her belly, the pangs of hunger. That is where hunger is, in front. She never looks back now. What does she possess, that she need fear to lose it on the way? The hair that grows in place of her old hair is soft and fluffy like swansdown. She will never have real hair again. The dead hair, roots and all, is scattered on the ground at Pursat. For ever more she will look like a grubby Buddhist nun.

She is beginning to know her way about. She knows where the sheltered places are. She recognizes the milestones along the road, and the gaping cavities in the rock face of the mountain, some pink, some green. Every night, she returns to the gravel pit, which is sheltered and dry. There are fewer mosquitoes there than near the river. Here, the heat of the sun is less intense. Here, she can lie in the shade with her eyes wide open, looking up at the glaring sky. She sleeps.

From her shelter in the gravel pit, she watches the rain. At irregular intervals, the reverberation of an explosion reaches her from the marble mountain, and a dense cloud of crows is hurled into the sky. Each day the water level rises among the clumps of bamboo on the banks of the Stung Pursat. Dogs slink past the gravel pit. They do not growl. They do not stop. She calls out to them, but they slink away. She says to herself: I am a girl who no longer smells of food.

She vomits, she retches, hoping to bring up the child, to root it out, but all she brings up is sour mango juice. She sleeps a great deal. She has become a sleeper, but it is not enough: night and day, the child continues to devour her. She feels and hears it nibbling incessantly in her belly. It erodes her body. It devours the flesh of her thighs, her arms, her cheeks. She touches them, and finds hollows where there used to be plumpness in the days of Tonle Sap. The child

8

has devoured everything, even the roots of her hair. Little by little, it is elbowing her out. The only thing it has not taken from her is her hunger. During sleep, the corroding acid in the pit of her stomach rises before her like a blazing red sun.

She discovers that, imperceptibly, changes have been taking place. She is beginning to see herself in relation to the external world. She realizes that she is, in some sense, growing internally. Rents appear in the surrounding darkness. A little light is admitted. This is what she has discovered: I am a very young girl, thin, with a belly so distended that the skin is beginning to crack. My great belly sags above my emaciated thighs. I am a very thin girl. I am going to have a child, and I have been driven out of my home.

She sleeps: I am someone who sleeps.

She is woken by the fire in her belly. There are flames leaping in the pit of her stomach. She vomits blood. No more sour mangoes for her, only rice-shoots. She searches. Mother Nature, give me a knife with which to kill this rat. The ground is barren. It bears nothing but pebbles worn smooth by the river. She turns over, lying on her stomach among the pebbles. The nibbling ceases, ceases, ceases altogether. She is suffocating. She raises herself up. The nibbling starts again.

Beyond the gap at the entrance to the gravel pit, the Stung Pursat is still rising.

It is brim-full, level with the ground on either side.

It is overflowing. Yellowish water sweeps away the clumps of bamboo. The dead branches drift gently downstream. She stares at the yellow waters. Her eyes become fixed. She feels as though they were nailed to their sockets. All feeling drains away as she stares at the drowning bamboo trees. Her hunger, too, is drowning in something more powerful than itself. Dispossession. She must find a way of dispossessing herself of everything. Eyes still fixed upon the drowning bamboos: it

9

is as though she believed those swollen waters could allay her hunger. But she has dreams in which, very suddenly for a moment or two, hunger returns to crush her. The girl's hunger is too much for her. It is like a great wave threatening to sweep her out of existence. She cries out. She tries to keep her eyes averted from the Stung Pursat. No, no, I haven't forgotten, I am here where my hands are.

From time to time, fishermen go past the gravel pit. One or two notice her. Most of them do not spare her a second glance. We had a neighbour in Tonle Sap who was a fisherman. I went into the forest with him. I am too young to understand. She eats young, budding vegetation, the tender shoots of banana trees. She watches the fishermen, to and fro, to and fro. She smiles at them. Gradually, a different rhythm of life establishes itself in the gravel pit, different from the rhythm of life outside. Except in snatches, as when she cuts her foot on a sharp splinter of marble, she tends to forget how it all began, she tends to forget that they drove her out because she was a fallen woman. She has, it seems to her, fallen from a great height, from the top of a tall tree, painlessly. She has fallen pregnant.

Her mother said: 'Don't give me that about your age. All right, you're only fourteen, or is it seventeen? We've all been young in our time. Be silent! We know all there is to know.' But, if what she meant was that she could still remember what is was like to be that age, it was a lie. Has anyone ever told you that there is mud in the region of Pursat, that one can eat, squatting under the open sky? That the spectacle of great areas of land flooded by the Stung Pursat is such as to hale one's soul out of one's body? One day, perhaps, I shall describe to you the explosions in the quarries, and the crows scattering in the sky. For I shall see you again. I must, since we are both living, you and I, and I have a lifetime before me. Who else but you should hear the tale I have to

tell? Who else does it concern that now I long for the food I cannot have more than I long for you? For days and weeks, hour upon hour, she contemplates and worships the food she cannot have. There is something that must be said to that ignorant peasant who drove her out. One day she will go back just to say it, just to say: I have forgotten you.

Then, one day, the child's hunger drives her out of the gravel pit. The sun is setting as she approaches the flickering lights of Pursat. She has been looking towards these lights for a long time now, but, so far, has never dared to venture near them. Yet, it was because of the lights, which she could see from the gravel pit, that she chose to remain there. Lights mean food. Tonight, the child's hunger is such that it is driving her towards the lights.

She is walking through the streets of the little town. She lingers in front of a market-stall, then walks on. The stall was unattended for a minute or two, and during that time she stole a salted fish. She slipped it down the front of her dress, between her breasts, and now she is taking it back to the gravel pit. On her way out of the town, she is stopped by a man, who asks her where she comes from. She says: 'From Battambang,' and takes to her heels. The man follows her, laughing. Turned out? Yes. They both laugh at the spectacle of her swollen belly. She is reassured. It was not on account of the fish that he spoke to her. He had not seen her take it.

'Battambang.'

The three syllables boom tonelessly, as though rapped out on a small, over-stretched drum. Baattamambbanangg. The man says that he has heard tell of it. She slips away.

Battambang. She has nothing else to say. On the way back to the gravel pit, she sinks her teeth in the fish, which is gritty with salt and dust. Late that night, she creeps out of the pit, and washes the fish with great care. Slowly, she eats it. Her gorge rises. Saliva pours into her mouth. The salt

brings tears to her eyes. She dribbles. She has not tasted salt for a long time. It is too much for her, much too much. She falls to the ground, and lying there, finishes every morsel of the nourishing food.

She sleeps. She wakes in pitch darkness to make a strange discovery: the child has devoured the fish. That too has been taken from her. She lies very still, realizing that tonight her hunger will be greater than ever before. What more will hunger drive her to do, that she would not otherwise have done? I shall go back to Battambang for a bowl of steaming rice, then I shall leave for ever. She wants a bowl of steaming rice, she wants it. She speaks the words aloud: 'warm rice.' Nothing happens. She takes a fistful of earth, and crams it in her mouth. Later, she wakes again, having forgotten what she did earlier. She does not understand. That fistful of earth might almost have been a bowl of steaming rice.

This is the first time that she has woken twice in the night.

There will be more such nights before the birth of the child. On one such night, long after she has reached the Mekong River, she will wander away from it in a state of torpor, and wake to find herself in a forest. Not in Calcutta, no, never in Calcutta. There will be no mistaking a handful of earth for food there. By the time she gets to Calcutta, everything will go like clockwork. By then, she will have lost her wits. The course of her life will be determined not by her but by some other agency.

A fisherman comes to the gravel pit, then another. The infant obstructs them. Little rat! It is high time he was out of there. With the money she gets from the fishermen, she goes several times to Pursat. She buys rice, which she cooks in an old tin can. They give her matches. She has hot rice to eat. The child is almost full-grown. The old hunger has gone, never to return.

The murky light of Pursat blots out the Cardamom Hills, the pencil-line horizon of Tonle Sap, the Stung Pursat, the winches grinding in the quarries. It lulls the unwary to sleep, writes Peter Morgan, an uneasy sleep, troubled by hideous dreams.

She wakes, looks about her, remembers where she is. She realizes that this murky light will last for six months at least. She cannot see the mountains now, nor the pencil-line horizon of her homeland. This morning she is carrying the child very low. She gets up, comes out of the gravel pit, and walks away from it into the murky light of the monsoon.

Of late, the fishermen have avoided her, sickened at the sight of her bald head—she now has almost no hair—and her emaciated body, deformed by the grossly swollen belly.

The old hunger will never return, she is sure of that. She knows that she must be very near her time. Very soon, the child will separate itself from her. That's it. It moves hardly at all now. It is ready, gathering that last ounce of strength which it needs to force its way out, to leave her.

She moves on, seeking a birthplace for the child, a hole somewhere, searching for someone to take up the child when it is born, and sever it from her completely. She seeks her worn-out mother, who drove her from her home. On no account are you to come back, ever. That woman did not know, she did not know everything. Nothing can stop me from coming back to you today, not if it means a thousand-mile journey over the mountains. You will be stupefied. You

13

will be too stunned to kill me, vile woman though you are, author of all my misery. I shall bring this child back to you, and you will take it. I shall throw it at your feet and run away, never to return. Under this pall of murky light, some things will come to an end, and others will begin. She must have her mother, her mother, as midwife at this birth. And perhaps she too will be released by this birth, a girl re-born, a bird on the wing, a budding sinner?

All the women for miles around Pursat are in flight, as she is, to escape from the glare of the summer monsoon, to give birth, or for some other reasons, such as the need to sleep.

She has not forgotten the directions given her by the old man. She follows the Stung Pursat upstream. She walks at night. She does not care to grope her way through the heat-laden fog. She cannot endure it. If anyone can tell me whether to kill the child or let it live, it is you. Her call for help is borne on waves of murky light. Mother, oh! mother. She is a child again, dependent as a child.

She walks.

For a whole week, she walks. The old hunger is gone, never to return.

Here, unmistakably, is the great lake of her homeland. Sudden fear brings her to a standstill. Wearily, her mother will watch her from the door of the straw hut. That look of utter weariness on her mother's face: still alive? I felt sure you must be dead. That is the thing she dreads most of all, the look in her mother's eyes, when she sees her banished child coming towards her.

For a whole day she hesitates, sheltering in a herdsman's hut on the lake shore, paralysed with dread of those reproachful eyes.

But, the following night, she does it. She goes upstream along the Tonle Sap, yes. Yes, she does the opposite of what the old man advised. She does it. Oh! surely her mother

must know that it is her right. If not, she will soon learn. With a cane in her hand, she will bar the door. She will recognize her, but will refuse to let her in. But this time, watch out for yourself!

To see her once more, then vanish into the monsoon. To render up the child to her.

She walks all through the night, and the whole of the following day. Through rice-fields, rice-fields. The sky is low overhead. From the time the sun rises, it is as though she were carrying a lead weight on her head. There is water everywhere. The sky is so low that it seems to press down on the rice-fields. Everything looks unfamiliar. She goes on.

She hurries on, faster and faster, filled with ever-increasing dread.

One morning she wakes, finds herself on the outskirts of a meat-market, and goes towards it. She recognizes the familiar smells of local cooking. This is her village, then. She has found her way home. She goes forward.

Squatting in the shade of a straw hut, which commands an excellent view of the square, she watches and waits. She is used to squatting like this in a village square, waiting for the market to end. But today is different. Today, she is there for a purpose, and she sees what she has come to see.

Her parents, approaching from the other side of the square. Because the sight of them is more than she can bear, she prostrates herself reverently. She remains so for a long time. When at last she dares to look up, she sees her mother smiling at her across the square.

This is not madness yet. Hunger, which of late had given way to fear, is rising in her again. The sight of meat, the smell of soup, have gone to her head. She babbles of her love for her mother. She imagines she smells incense, sees fireworks exploding. She talks to herself. She thanks God. The market place seems to be spinning round at dizzying speed.

Such sparkle, such gaiety!

She sees her brothers and sisters perched on top of a cart. She waves to them. They point and laugh. They have recognized her. She prostrates herself once more, and remains with her forehead touching the ground. There is a loaf on the ground in front of her. Who could have laid it there for her? Who but her mother?

She eats, and there and then, in the corner of the square close by the straw hut, she lies down and sleeps.

She wakes in the searing, livid glare of sunlight, which reaches to every corner of the now deserted square. The market has vanished. Where are her people? Is it possible that they have given her the slip? She is sure she remembers hearing her mother say: 'It's time we went home.'

But was it her mother? Or was it some other woman, not really her mother, who saw that she was in danger, recognized the signs, the swollen belly, and said that it was time for her to go home?

She stayed in the corner of the square until nightfall. A woman brought her a bowl of rice. She is utterly bewildered. Who was it who decreed: 'We must go home, but you must not come with us?'

She sleeps all afternoon, crushed, as she was in the foothills of the Cardamoms. At dusk, she wakes. She is confused. The thought comes to her that perhaps the woman she saw was not really her mother, nor the crowd of children really her brothers and sisters. How could she be sure that she had seen her real mother, her real brothers and sisters? After all this time, could she really expect to be able to tell the difference between this family and that?

At nightfall, she begins retracing her steps, following the course of the Tonle Sap, as the old man had directed her.

She will never be seen again in her native region.

Under the white, searing sun, with the child still in her

16

womb, she leaves her homeland. She is fearless, now. Her way is clear before her. Her mother has pronounced sentence of exile, from which there is no appeal. Tears stream down her face, but she pays no heed to them. She is singing, singing at the top of her voice, one of the songs she learnt as a child in the village of Battambang.

Peter Morgan has stopped writing.

He leaves his room, and walks across the Embassy grounds towards the broad avenue which runs beside the Ganges.

There she is, opposite the residence of the former Vice-Consul of France in Lahore. In the shade of an overhanging bush, her dress of coarse sacking still sopping wet, she lies asleep. Her bald head is shaded by the bush. Peter Morgan knows that she has spent part of the night swimming and hunting for food in the Ganges, and the rest accosting passers-by in the streets, and singing. This is how she spends her nights. Peter Morgan has followed her through the streets of Calcutta. This is what he knows.

Close to her recumbent body are the bodies of the lepers.

The lepers are waking.

Peter Morgan is young. He wants to shoulder the misery of Calcutta. He wants to plunge into its depths. He wants to do it now, to get it over, so that wisdom may start to grow out of bitter experience.

It is seven o'clock in the morning, shadowy as dusk. A motionless pall of cloud hangs over Nepal.

Already, slowly at first, Calcutta is beginning to stir. A swarming ants' nest, thinks Peter Morgan. Dinginess, horror, the fear of God, misery and yet more misery, he thinks.

Nearby, shutters creak. They are the Vice-Consul's. He is getting up. Peter Morgan makes a dash for the Embassy grounds, takes refuge behind the iron railings, and waits.

The Vice-Consul of France in Lahore appears, half-dressed, on his balcony. He glances quickly up and down the avenue, then returns indoors. Peter Morgan crosses the grounds of the French Embassy. He is returning to the residence of his friends, the Stretters.

An unwholesome-looking sky in the morning ensures that white residents, unused to the climate of Calcutta, will wake up looking liverish. He himself does, he notices, as he examines his reflection in the mirror.

He goes out on to the balcony of his residence.

Today, at seven o'clock in the morning, it is shadowy as dusk in Calcutta. Motionless clouds, like a great mountain range, hang over Nepal. Below the clouds, a layer of foul, stagnant mist. In a day or two, the city will be drowning in the summer monsoon. In the shade of an overhanging bush, opposite the Vice-Consul's residence, she lies sleeping on sandy ground, with her bald head in the shade of the bush. She spent part of the night swimming and hunting for food, and the rest in singing and accosting passers-by in the streets.

Rotary water-sprinklers spray the streets, turning the dust into a damp paste, which gives off the stench of urine.

The grey pilgrims have already begun immersing themselves in the Ganges. The lepers, as always, wake one by one, and watch from the banks.

For the past two hours, a pitiful swarm of men and women have been toiling in the mills of Calcutta, earning the bare means of survival.

The Vice-Consul of Lahore surveys Calcutta, the smoking chimneys, the Ganges, the water-sprinklers, the sleeping woman. Even at this hour it is unbearably hot. He goes indoors and, after shaving, contemplates his greying temples in the mirror. He has shaved. Well, that's done. He goes out

on to the balcony again, and, once more, surveys the buildings and the palm trees, the water-sprinklers, the sleeping
woman, the hordes of lepers on the river banks, the pilgrims.
Such is the stuff of Calcutta, or Lahore, palm trees, lepers,
a pall of cloud and mist blotting out the sky.

The Vice-Consul takes a shower, gulps down his morning
coffee, and settles himself on a couch to read a letter which
has just arrived from France. In the dusky light of early
morning, he reads his aunt's letter. One windy night last
month an unprecedented mishap occurred at the little house
in Paris: a shutter was blown open, as well as the window,
which had been left open a crack to air the place. Having
been notified by the police, she went to the house the following afternoon, to lock up and check that everything was in
order. The house had not been burgled. Oh! yes, and another
thing, it had almost slipped her mind: all the lilac bushes
near the railings had been stripped; no one there to look
after them. It was always the same, year after year, in the
spring, girls stealing the lilac. Savages!

Tomorrow night, Friday, there is to be a reception at the
French Embassy. At the last minute, the Vice-Consul received
an invitation. Suddenly he remembers something, the note
from the Ambassador's wife, which was delivered last night:
'Come.'

He gets up, goes out to tell his Indian manservant to brush
his dinner jacket, and returns to the couch. He has finished
reading the letter from his aunt, who lives in the Malsherbes
district. He re-reads the passages relating to the broken
shutter and the lilac bushes, and makes a mental note: the
letter has been duly read.

He sits with the letter in his hand, waiting until it is time
to leave for the office. Thus, in his mind's eye, he sees the
drawing-room. Everything is in order. The black grand
piano is shut. On the music-stand there is a score, also shut,

whose title, 'Indiana's Song', he cannot read. The padlock on the gate is double-locked. No one can get into the garden. No risk of anyone creeping near enough to read the title on the score. On the piano stands a Chinese vase converted into a lamp. It has a shade of green silk, forty years old, is it? Yes. Had it stood there before the birth of him who was born there, then? Yes. There is a lull. The shutter has been left open. The green lampshade is bathed in bright sunlight. People stop at the gate: something will have to be done, or there will be no getting any sleep tonight. Didn't you hear the dismal racket it made all last night? More people stop. There is quite a little crowd gathered: who owns this house, which is kept permanently locked up? A single man, about thirty-five years of age.

His name is Jean-Marc de H.

An only son. An orphan now.

The little house in Paris, with garden all around, still spoken of as a 'private residence', is kept locked up for years on end, because its owner is abroad in the Consular Service. At present in India. The police know whom to notify in any emergency such as this, or in the event of fire: an old lady who lives in the Malsherbes district, the absent owner's aunt.

The wind has risen again. The shutter swings to. The sunlight recedes, leaving the green silk in shadow. The piano is shrouded in darkness, and will remain so until the end of its owner's tour of duty. Two years.

Doubtless, the sound of stiff bristles on the tough fabric of a dinner jacket is one with which the Vice-Consul is not yet wholly familiar. He gets up and shuts the door.

Now it is time to go to the office, as, earlier, it was time to get up.

The Vice-Consul covers the short distance on foot, a ten-minute walk, along the Ganges, past the trees in whose

shade the joyful lepers wait, across the Embassy gardens with their oleanders and palm trees, to the Consulate, a building surrounded by a wall, inside the grounds.

In the garden, a voice can still be faintly heard asking: When the gentleman is at home, do you ever hear music played on the piano? Scales? A tune clumsily played with one hand? The voice of someone very old replies: Yes, long ago, at night, yes, a child used to pick out with one finger a tune that sounded like 'Indiana's Song'. And more recently? The old, quavering voice replies: Yes, in the past, more recently, the sound of things being smashed, mirrors most likely, could be heard at night in the house where the man lived alone, the man who as a child had played 'Indiana's Song'. That was all.

As he walks, the Vice-Consul whistles 'Indiana's Song'. Charles Rossett, emerging from behind a row of trees, comes upon him so suddenly that, this time, he cannot avoid an encounter. They exchange a few words. The Vice-Consul announces that he has been invited to tomorrow's reception at the Embassy. Charles Rossett is scarcely able to conceal his astonishment. This, says the Vice-Consul, will be the first reception he has attended in Calcutta, and it will probably also be his last. Charles Rossett hurries away, pleading urgent business. He goes on towards the offices of the Embassy.

It is five weeks since Jean-Marc de H. came to a town on the banks of the Ganges which we will call Calcutta, principal city of India, whose population remains constant at five million, as does the number—unknown—of those dying of hunger who enter the city daily, a city plunged today in the murky gloom of the summer monsoon.

He has come from Lahore, where he served with the rank of Vice-Consul for a year and a half, and from where he was recalled, following incidents distressing to his superiors in

23

the Diplomatic Service in Calcutta. He is waiting here for his next posting. There are difficulties. The matter is hanging fire. Bombay has been mentioned, but nothing has yet been decided. It was considered advisable by his superiors to keep him occupied during his stay in Calcutta. As is usual in such cases, he is attached to the records office. The house where he is staying is Embassy property, kept for the use of junior staff posted to Calcutta.

While rumours of the incidents in Lahore have reached the ears of everyone in Calcutta, no one, except Monsieur Stretter and his wife, knows the details.

The Vice-Consul's whistling of 'Indiana's Song' ceases abruptly.

In Calcutta, in the murky light of early morning, he has just caught sight of Anne-Marie Stretter crossing the Embassy grounds.

She goes into one of the outbuildings. She reaffirms that all surplus food must be given to the starving poor of Calcutta. From now on, she says, in addition to the scraps of food, a bowl of drinking water must be put out at the back gate behind the kitchens, because they will need fresh water to drink, now that the monsoon has begun.

Having given her orders, Anne-Marie Stretter retraces her steps. Her daughters are waiting for her in one of the tree-lined walks. They go towards the tennis courts, but before they get there, they turn down a side path, and can be seen in the distance strolling through the grounds. It is already too hot. For the past few days, the tennis courts have been deserted. They are dressed in white shorts and sleeveless blouses. As for her, she is bare-headed. She is not afraid of the sun. The Vice-Consul of Lahore has passed beyond the Embassy buildings when Anne-Marie Stretter sees him. She nods. Like everyone else in Calcutta, she treats him with reserve. He bows and walks on. They have been meeting in

this way for the past five weeks, and their acquaintance has not progressed beyond a nod and a bow.

A woman's bicycle is propped up against the wire netting which surrounds the deserted tennis courts. It belongs to Anne-Marie Stretter.

The French Ambassador has invited Charles Rossett to assist him in his examination of the file of Jean-Marc de H.

In the Ambassador's office, the blinds are drawn to exclude the murky day. The lights are switched on. They are alone.

Charles Rossett reads out to the Ambassador Jean-Marc de H.'s written statement regarding the incidents in Lahore.

'I served a year and a half as Vice-Consul in Lahore,' Charles Rossett reads. 'I applied for a posting to India four years ago, and when it came through, I accepted it without reservations. I do not deny the facts as stated regarding my conduct in Lahore. I have no doubt that the statements of witnesses were made in good faith, excepting that of my Indian servant. I accept full responsibility for my actions.

'My superiors, upon whom my future depends, must proceed as they think fit. If they find it necessary to dismiss me, I shall accept their ruling, as I shall also if they decide to retain me in the Consular Service. I am prepared to go anywhere. I do not ask to be reinstated in Lahore, nor to be relieved of my post there. I cannot go into the reasons for my conduct at Lahore, nor explain why I feel obliged to remain silent on this subject. I do not believe that anything I could say would be of interest either to the Department or to any outside agency. I trust that my refusal to speak will not be misunderstood. I suspect no one. I condemn no one. I can do no more at this stage than simply assert that I find it

impossible to give an account, in terms that would be understood, of what took place in Lahore.

'I must add, in conclusion, that I was not, as has been suggested, under the influence of drink, when I acted as I did in Lahore.'

'I was expecting he would tender his resignation,' says the Ambassador, 'but he hasn't done so.'

'When are you seeing him?'

'I don't know yet.'

The Ambassador looks with a kindly eye upon Charles Rossett.

'I have no right to ask you, I know, but I should be grateful for your help in clearing up this unhappy business.'

Jean-Marc de H.'s personal file yields the following information: Only child; Father: branch-manager of a small bank, deceased; Mother: also deceased, two years ago. There had been a stepfather, a recording engineer in Brest. Small private residence in Neuilly kept on by Jean-Marc de H., and occupied by him when on leave. Education: A year as a boarder in a secondary school at Montfort, Seine-et-Oise, between the ages of 13 and 14. Said to be a delicate child, requiring plenty of good fresh air. Early scholastic attainments: average. Scholastic attainments at Montfort: outstanding. Expelled from Montfort for unsatisfactory conduct. Nature of misconduct not specified. From there, returned to Paris and attended another secondary school. Nothing further to report on school life.

The file throws little light, either, on his career since the fulfilment of his ambition to enter the Foreign Service. Following three successive requests for leave of absence on half-pay, Jean-Marc de H. was away from Paris for four years. There is no record of why these requests were made, nor of where he went. His personal reports classify him as average. It would seem that Jean-Marc de H. waited until

he got to India to reveal himself in his true colours. One striking omission: the absence, to all appearances, of any entanglements with women.

The Ambassador wrote to the only surviving relation, an aunt living in the Malsherbes district of Paris. She replied at great length by return of post. 'So there must have been latent in this child,' she commented, 'things which we, who believed we knew him, were far from suspecting. Who would have thought it?'

'Is it suggested that he is insane?'

'No, only that he is suffering from nervous depression. In spite of the fact that he did it repeatedly, they still went on believing it was just a brainstorm.'

There were no complaints until very late in the day.

'At first,' the Ambassador goes on to explain, 'he was treated as something of a joke, a harmless, trigger-happy crank. And then he took to screaming in the night . . . and then—it must be said—corpses were found in the Shalimar Gardens.'

What had the Malsherbes aunt to say about his childhood? Nothing much: he seemed to prefer boarding school to the comforts of home. It was that year in Montfort that changed him, she said. On his return home he seemed more reserved, almost hardened, one might say. All the same, no one could have foreseen what was to happen in Lahore. In other words, nothing in the least abnormal, except perhaps the absence of women in his life, and even there how could one be sure?

Charles Rossett reads on:

'I do not know of any woman with whom my nephew may have been on friendly terms. I am very sorry I cannot help you there, but he always preferred his own company, and has continued to live alone, in spite of all our efforts. From an early age, he kept us—his mother and me—at

arm's length and, needless to say, never took us into his confidence, even in little things. For my sake and for the sake of his mother's memory, I beg you, sir, to view the case in the kindest possible light. Admittedly, my nephew behaved like a madman in Lahore, but, when all is said and done, could this not perhaps point to some hidden emotional disturbance which eludes us, but which may not be entirely discreditable? Before condemning his conduct out of hand, would it not perhaps be advisable to go into it further, to probe in depth? Why go back to his childhood for an explanation of his conduct in Lahore? Should not enquiries also be made on the spot?'

'I prefer to follow the normal procedure, and investigate the childhood background,' says the Ambassador.

He extracts the letter from the file.

'I would rather not pass this on to Lahore,' he says. 'I fear it would be extremely damaging. It's irregular, and that's why I felt I ought to tell you. What do you think?'

Charles Rossett, with some hesitation, admits to being puzzled. Why is everyone so ready to make allowances for Jean-Marc de H.? Surely this is a case for exemplary punishment?

'If it were less serious, yes,' says the Ambassador. 'In this case, there is no plaintiff, do you see, it's a . . . situation . . . that's obvious, and Lahore . . . who cares about Lahore?'

Does he ever see him? the Ambassador asks. No, no one here sees him, except for that sot, the Secretary of the European Club. As far as anyone knows, he had not a single friend in Lahore.

'He confides in the Club Secretary,' says Charles Rossett, 'although he must know that almost every word he says is passed on.'

'Does he talk about Lahore?'

'No. Mostly about his childhood, apparently, as you hoped . . .'

'But why do you think he does it?'

Charles Rossett has no idea.

'His work is irreproachable,' the Ambassador says. 'He seems to have returned to normal. What shall we do with him?'

The two men ponder the problem of what to do with Jean-Marc de H. Where should they send him? What surroundings, what climate would best protect him from himself?

'When he was asked, apparently he mentioned Bombay. But they won't want him in Bombay. There's always Calcutta. I could keep him here. But Calcutta, after a time, can be worse than most places.'

'I have the impression that he doesn't find it as . . . impossible as, for instance, we might,' Charles Rossett says. 'Oddly enough, Calcutta seems to suit him.'

A sudden storm blows up. Almost before the Ambassador has time to cross to the window and raise the blind, it is over. The sun appears briefly in a patch of clear sky, then disappears as the dense clouds coagulate once more. There is a hush in the garden, where the storm-clouds have blotted out the shadows.

The Vice-Consul's invitation to the forthcoming reception is discussed by the two men. Did Madame Stretter send the invitation only after reading the letter from the Malsherbes aunt? Why leave it to the last minute? Had she reservations even then?

'I daresay she felt that a note written in her own hand at the last minute,' the Ambassador says, 'would make him feel personally wanted, and, as a result, he would be sure to come. My wife and I, you know, are anxious, as far as is consistent with protocol, not to exclude anyone, however strong a case there may seem to be for doing so.'

The Ambassador turns his searching gaze on Charles Rossett.

'You're finding it hard to settle down, aren't you?'

Charles Rossett smiles.

'Somewhat harder than I expected.'

'You should go out to the Islands,' advises Monsieur Stretter. 'It's essential to get into the habit, if you mean to stick it out in Calcutta.'

He himself prefers to get right away from Calcutta. He goes shooting in Nepal. His wife will be going to the Islands, and their daughters will follow in a week or so, when their classes end. If only for the sake of spending a couple of days in the fabulous Prince of Wales Hotel, it is worth going. Furthermore, the journey from Calcutta to the Delta is of great interest. The experience of driving through the vast rice-fields of the Delta, the granary of Northern India, is one that should not be missed. One must see for oneself India's archaic agriculture, one must learn more of India. One should never miss a chance of seeing the country in which one happens to be. It does not do to confine oneself to Calcutta. Why should not Charles Rossett go this very weekend? It is the first weekend of the summer monsoon. By Saturday afternoon, the day after tomorrow, there will scarcely be an Englishman or Frenchman left in Calcutta.

Having said his say, the Ambassador beckons Charles Rossett over to the window.

The Vice-Consul can be seen coming across the grounds towards them. He turns to stare at the deserted tennis courts, then walks on. He goes past the open window, and, for all the notice he takes, it might as well not be there.

Other people come out of the Consulate and walk across the grounds. It is midday. No one approaches or speaks to him.

'It must be five weeks that he's been waiting for me to send

for him,' says the Ambassador. 'I can't keep putting it off much longer.'

But is he really impatient for this summons? Or is he perhaps hoping that it will be deferred, indefinitely deferred? No one knows.

The Ambassador, smiling with some constraint, says:

'We have a delightful young English friend staying with us at the moment. He can't stand the sight of the Vice-Consul of Lahore. . . . It's not that he's exactly afraid of him, it's just that the man makes him feel uncomfortable. Yes, people do avoid him, one must admit. . . . I'm inclined to myself.'

Charles Rossett, having taken his leave of the Ambassador, is now, in his turn, crossing the grounds. The Nepalese palm trees, which cast no shadows, are motionless.

In the avenue which runs beside the Ganges, Charles Rossett sees the Vice-Consul.

He has stopped to stare at the lepers as, earlier, he did at the tennis courts.

Charles Rossett hesitates, the heat is so intense, but, all the same, in the end he turns back. Once more, he crosses the grounds, goes out by the other gate, and walks to his residence, which is in the same avenue as the Vice-Consul's, but further from the Embassy. It is identical in every respect, a bungalow with a verandah, of flaking yellow stucco, surrounded by oleanders.

'Do have a word with him, that is, of course, unless you really feel you can't face it,' the Ambassador said.

Charles Rossett takes a shower, his second that day. Water from the underground springs of Calcutta is invariably cool.

The table is laid. Charles Rossett unfolds his napkin and

eats his meal of Indian curry. The curry is hot. It is always too hot here. Charles Rossett forces it down as though it were a penance.

Then, as soon as he has finished eating, Charles Rossett goes to his darkened bedroom, and sleeps.

It is half-past one.

Charles Rossett surrenders himself with his whole being to sleep, gaining hours on the merciless daylight of Calcutta. He has been sleeping in this way for the past five weeks.

Anyone walking in the avenue in the crushing heat of early afternoon would see the Vice-Consul, all but naked, pacing up and down his bedroom in what appears to be a state of intense wakefulness.

It is three o'clock in the afternoon.

An Indian servant wakes Charles Rossett. A face with a sly expression peers cautiously through the open door. It is time for the master to wake up. He opens his eyes. As always in the afternoon, he had forgotten, he had forgotten Calcutta. This room is dark. Does the master wish for tea? We have been dreaming of a rosy-cheeked woman, a rosy-cheeked reader who reads Proust in the bitter gales of a far-off Channel port. Does the master wish for tea? Is the master unwell? We dreamt that, in the presence of this rosy-cheeked woman who reads, we experienced a degree of confusion somehow relating to this world here, to the shadowy form of a woman in white shorts, walking with tranquil step every day in the dusky light of morning, past the tennis courts, which are deserted because of the summer monsoon.

Yes, bring tea. And open the shutters.

There. The shutters open with a grating sound. They will never learn how to handle them. Where do they need oiling?

Light reverberates round the room, blindingly. And with

the light comes nausea. Every day there is this urge to telephone the Ambassador: 'Your Excellency, I must request a transfer. I cannot, I simply cannot stand Calcutta.'

Or would it be better to wait for love to come to the rescue?

The electric fan is switched on. The servant has gone back to the kitchen to get tea. He leaves behind him a smell of cotton garments and dust. We are imprisoned together in the Consular Residence for three more years.

Charles Rossett has gone back to sleep.

The servant returns with the tea, peers to make sure that he is still alive, wakes him.

There are a white shirt and dinner jacket to be pressed before tomorrow. For the reception at the French Embassy tomorrow night, of course.

The man in Lahore, Charles Rossett recalls, the Vice-Consul's Indian servant, fled rather than testify against his master. He was caught, and he told lies.

Charles Rossett gets up, takes a shower, goes out on to his verandah, and sees a black Lancia coming out through the Embassy gates. It turns into the avenue. With Anne-Marie Stretter is an Englishman whom he has seen once or twice before on the tennis courts.

The black Lancia gathers speed and disappears. So it is probably true, what they say about her.

Did Charles Rossett feel he wanted positive proof? No doubt he did.

He goes into the kitchen quarters and drinks brandy with ice in it, while his white shirt is being pressed according to instructions.

Charles Rossett returns once more across the Embassy grounds in the unremitting heat. His thoughts turn to the people he will meet at the reception tomorrow night. He will dance with the women in strict order of precedence. He

will ask Anne-Marie Stretter to dance. At this moment, she is on the road to Chandernagore. In this heat.

He catches sight of the Vice-Consul, some way off. He sees him emerge from the avenue of oleanders and take a step or two towards the tennis courts. At this end of the grounds, there is no one about except Charles Rossett and Jean-Marc de H.

Jean-Marc de H. does not know that Charles Rossett is watching him. He believes himself to be alone. Charles Rossett checks his stride. He hopes to get a look at the Vice-Consul's face, but the Vice-Consul has his back to him, and does not turn round. Leaning against the wire netting that surrounds the tennis courts is a woman's bicycle.

It is not the first time, Charles Rossett at once realizes, that he has seen this bicycle there.

The Vice-Consul leaves the path, and goes over to the bicycle.

He is up to something. It is hard to make out, at this distance, exactly what he is doing. He seems to be peering at the bicycle, touching it. He stands bent over it for a long time, then straightens up and goes on staring at it.

He walks back to the avenue, lurching slightly, but unhurried. He makes for the Consulate, and disappears inside.

Charles Rossett, in his turn, makes for the tennis courts. The bicycle, propped up against the wire netting, is coated with fine greyish dust, from the drive.

It is abandoned, unwanted, frightening.

Charles Rossett walks away hurriedly. On his way, he passes a stranger. They look at one another. Does he know, this stranger? No. Does all Calcutta know? All Calcutta is keeping silent. Or does not know.

Why does the Vice-Consul go out of his way morning and evening, every day, to the tennis courts? What is he up to?

Whom should he tell? Whom should he talk to about this? How can he mention it to anyone? It is impossible to put into words.

The avenue, once again, is deserted. The stranger has left the grounds. The air shimmers before his eyes. Charles Rossett attempts to conjure up the smooth face of the Vice-Consul, and finds that he no longer has the power to do so.

Someone, hidden from sight, whistles 'Indiana's Song'.

The child was born near Udang, in a sheltered spot close to a smallholding that she had haunted for two days on account of the farmer's wife, because she too was thin and old. The woman had helped her. Two days running, she had brought her rice and fish soup and, on the third day, a jute sack for the journey, writes Peter Morgan.

She does not throw this girl child, this Siamese twin of hers, into the Mekong, nor leave it behind her on her way through the Rattan Valley. The other children born to her after this little girl she will abandon, always at the same hour, wherever she may be, in the middle of the day, when her head is buzzing and swimming from the glare of the sun. At nightfall, she will find herself alone. She will wonder what has become of that thing, fashioned in her own image, which, a moment ago, was in her arms, and which she should not have laid down—a moment's pause, and one finds oneself moving on without it. She will not be able to find it. She will scratch her breasts where a few drops of milk have collected, and move on. The first time she forgets, she may grieve perhaps. But the times after that, she will scarcely notice the difference. She walks on, and then she sleeps. Battambang, the shrill song of children perched on top of buffalo, swaying and laughing, she sings before she falls asleep in the jungle darkness. Brushwood fires ring the forest villages, but she is beyond them, where the tigers are.

After Udang the way, along the Tonle Sap, is easy. With

the child carried upright in the sack which is fastened to her shoulders and tied round her waist, she continues to follow the Tonle Sap downstream. At Pnom Penh she stops for several days. From there, she follows the Mekong River downstream, the Mekong, dotted with hundreds of junks bearing cargoes of rice to the other side.

A woman told her the way, after she left Pursat but before she reached Kompong Chnam, before the birth of the child. After Pnom Penh make for Chowdoc. She remembers. She cannot hope to get work while she has the child with her. No one would want her. Even before, she could not find work, a girl of seventeen with a distended belly. Wherever she went, she was driven out. Try further on.

She will never find work. She will never know what it is to work.

The woman gave her one useful hint: White people, it was said, could sometimes be persuaded to take in children and care for them. She sets off again. She does not seek further guidance. No one here speaks Cambodian. It is almost unheard of. The first white station? Be off! She must keep on following the Mekong. This, she knows, is the right way. She follows the Mekong. The child on her back sleeps nearly all the time. Lately, in the last week or two, especially in the last day or two, she has been sleeping a great deal. She has to be woken, to be fed. Fed on what? The child must have something, it is time. Then on again, feeling lighter, picking her way beside the rice-fields. Her eyes, ringed with bluish lids, are glazed. Has she ever once stopped to look at anything? At Lontsu Yen she sees white people here and there in the streets. A white station. She makes for the market place, spreads out a rag, lays the child down on it, and waits. A Cambodian woman, the last she is to meet on her journey, comes up to her and tells her that the child is dead. But she pinches the child, and it gives a cry. Of course it's not dead!

38

The Cambodian woman tells her that the child is dying. She'll have to hurry if . . .

'What do you mean to do with it?'

'Give it away.'

The woman taunts her: who would not be ashamed to be seen with it, a child as skinny as that? In Sadec she sees more whites. She makes for the market place, lays the child down on the piece of rag, and waits. No one says a word to her. The child is sleeping more than ever. Why not leave her there, asleep . . .? But what of the dogs over there on the other side of the market place? She moves on. In Vinh Long there are more white people, hordes of them!

She goes to the market place, and lays the child down on the piece of rag in front of her. She squats and waits. This particular market place sends her into gales of laughter. Sometimes, after long hours of walking—she has been pressing on rapidly of late, hoping to outstrip death—the sight of a market place makes her brain reel. The market at Vinh Long has this effect on her. Anyone who wants this beautiful baby can have it, she says, and for nothing, because she can't take it with her. Look at my foot, then you'll see why. No one understands. There is a wound on her foot, a long thin gash made by a sharp stone. Under the scab, worms are crawling. She does not notice the stench. The child sleeps. She does not look at it, nor at her foot, which is stretched out beside the child. She talks to herself as she did in that market place in Tonle Sap, where she saw her mother looking so preoccupied. She talks, intoxicated by the sight of so many good things to eat spread out on the market stalls, by the smell of roast meat and hot soup. Who will take this child? She has no more milk. This morning, the child refused even the few drops that remained. A bowl of hot rice was handed to her from one of the junks. She chewed the rice for a long time, and then dribbled it into the

39

baby's mouth, but the child brought it all up. Very well, then. There's nothing for it but to tell a barefaced lie. To say that the child is a healthy child. Whoever wants it has only to ask. She has been waiting two hours already. She does not realize that she has already left behind the people who understood her language. Yesterday she was aware of it, but not today.

It is not until the end of the day, after most of the stalls have been cleared, that a white woman passes by. She is fat and heavy, and is accompanied by a white child.

Understanding returns to the girl. With quick cunning, she sees her chance.

She sees, beneath the pith helmet, the eyes of a woman who is no longer young, looking. At last.

She did look.

She is the first. She smiles up at her. The woman comes nearer, takes a piastre from her purse, and gives it to the girl.

She moves off.

The girl calls after her, and beckons. The lady turns back. The girl points to the baby, and holds out the piastre. She turns round, points in the direction from which she has come, and cries: 'Battambang.' The lady stares, no, she is beginning to walk away, she refuses to take back the piastre. A little crowd has gathered round the shrieking girl.

The lady goes on her way.

The girl picks up her child, and runs after her. She overtakes her, and pours out a stream of words. She points this way and that, and, laughing, holds out the child. The lady, with an exclamation which the girl does not understand, pushes her aside. The white child who is with the lady looks at the baby as though she were . . . what? Well, what? She says something to the lady, who shakes her head. She walks away.

The girl, too, walks on. She follows the lady. The lady

40

turns and shoos her away. But, as against her dread of having to keep the child, nothing can frighten her.

The girl gives the lady time to take a few more steps, then she starts following her again, the piastre still in her hand. The lady turns and shouts at her, stamping her foot. The girl smiles back. She starts all over again, showing her foot, pointing to the north, holding out the baby, babbling. The lady walks on, ignoring her.

The girl, keeping her distance, follows her along the street, still holding out the baby and the piastre, still smiling. The lady does not turn round again.

The white child leaves her mother, and walks beside the girl.

The girl's chatter ceases. She catches up with the lady, whose child is tripping along beside her. Thus they walk in procession through the streets of the little town for an hour. The girl keeps silent, waiting outside shops with the white child, until the lady comes out. The girl and the white child are now inseparable. The white lady scolds her child, but the child does not cry. On the return journey the lady has a trio of followers. The chances of success are greater now. There is a look of determination on the face of the little white girl, which is more marked with every step they take. As they walk, the girl watches the little white child, who, in her turn, never takes her eyes off her mother's back, ahead of her. The lady turns round. The three behind her also turn round. If the woman were to shout or attempt to drive her off, all three might stand there silently, waiting, or close in and cling to her. They are at the gate. The girl realizes that nothing short of a hard slap will persuade the white child to leave her.

The lady is at the gate. She opens it and, with her hand still on the knob, turns and subjects her own child to a long, calculating look, weighing up the pros and cons. She is

blind to everything but the look in her daughter's eyes. She gives in.

The gate shuts once more. The girl and her baby are inside.

There can be no mistake about it: the thing has happened. Search as thoroughly as you will, she has n<u>ot</u> got the baby, writes Peter Morgan.

It is done: the child has been taken from her, and carried into the house.

Joyful song of Battambang, which proclaims that the buffalo will eat the grass, even though the grass in its turn, when the time is ripe, will swallow up the buffalo. It is afternoon. The girl, having attained her object, is resting in the garden, which is surrounded by walls and a hibiscus hedge. The house is painted white. There are no passers-by. She is sitting in the shade, her back resting against the smooth trunk of a custard-apple tree. Propped up against the tree, with support for her back. There are no passers-by. They shut the main gate after the little convoy went through. Flowers growing in beds. No stray dogs. There are custard-apples on the ground. Windfalls that burst as they hit the ground, exposing creamy pulp, thick as butter, which oozes into the dust. The lady made a sign to her to sit and wait. The girl is hopeful; if she were to give her back the baby, if she thought such a thing were possible, she would find no arms stretched out to receive it. Nothing. Emptiness. Hands pressed into the small of her back. To get her to stretch out her arms again, they would first have to break them. Escape! Slip through the hedge like a snake! No, there is nothing to fear. How quiet it is. No passers-by here. The custard-apples, the windfalls, ooze where they fall. Not

crushed underfoot. These people step aside to avoid them. Nothing to fear: the white child of the white lady wills it. God wills it. The baby has been given. It has been received. It is done.

The girl has come to the Plain of Birds.

She does not know this. The lady lives in the Plain of Birds, in the first white township of the region, but there is no possible means of communicating this information to the girl. There is no one who speaks her language. She is four hundred miles from Pursat. Has a year passed since her confinement? It must have taken place at Udang, then? Allowing for the fact that she progressed more slowly after Udang, because she could not walk so fast with that dragging burden on her back; allowing for time spent in searching for the means of survival, with men, on the outskirts of villages, begging and stealing, and the time wasted in sleep and looking about her, almost a year must have elapsed between her leaving Battambang and coming to rest here in this garden, in the Plain of Birds.

The Plain of Birds, also, will be left behind.

She will travel north for a short while and then, after some weeks, will turn westward. After that she will spend ten years on the road, travelling towards Calcutta. Calcutta, her journey's end. She will stop there. She stays, she is there, in the monsoon. There, in Calcutta, sleeping among the lepers, in the bushes on the banks of the Ganges.

Why that route rather than any other? Why? Was it the birds she was following, and not a route at all? Or the routes of the Chinese tea convoys of former times? No. Wherever she happened to find a path or foothold, whether among trees or on bare slopes, there she walked.

Two more white children, boys this time, come through the trees towards her. They stare at her for a little while, then skip their way through the custard-apples on the

44

ground, their feet shod in white sandals. The white lady's little girl does not reappear. A man, most probably a servant, brings her food: meat, fish, hot rice, laying it on the ground in front of her. She eats. Surely she should be able to see. At the opposite end of the drive from the gate there is a covered verandah. There are twenty yards of drive between her and the verandah. She is leaning against her custard-apple tree, with food in front of her, but she can see. The child, wrapped in white linen, is lying on a table. The lady is bending over her. On either side, her own children stand and watch in silence. The little white girl is there: there is a God, then. She sees the lady trying to give the baby milk from a little bottle. She pours it into her mouth. The lady shakes the child, and gives a shriek, and then another. The girl, with a twinge of fear, scrambles to her feet. The child, it seems, is ill. Can that mean that they will give it back to her, and drive her out? Would it not be safer to slip away now, at once? Of course not! Not one of them has even glanced at her. Oh! that child, how she can sleep! She manages to sleep through the lady's screams, just as she slept through the silence of a day's march. The lady starts again. She shakes the child, shrieks, pours milk into her. It's no use. The child will not drink. The milk trickles out of her mouth. None of it goes down her throat. Any spark of life that remains can do no more than resist all attempts to prolong it. There is a change. The lady puts down the bottle, and peers intently at the sleeping child. The little white children are still silent, still waiting; there are three of them now, wanting to keep her. God is everywhere. The lady takes the child in her arms. The child does not stir. The lady, still supporting its back, stands the child on the table. Its head droops to one side. It is still asleep. The child's belly is blown up like a balloon, filled with gas and worms. Once more, the lady lays the child on the tablecloth. She sits beside it in silence. Silently,

45

she broods. Another change: the lady, using two fingers, prises the child's mouth open, and sees what? Teeth, no doubt. What else should she see? The lady, seeming to stifle a cry, looks at the girl under the tree. Guiltily, the girl lowers her eyes. She waits. Is the danger past? No. Once again the lady puts the child down on the cloth, and comes towards her. What is she saying? It is so hard to understand. What can she want? She holds out her hands, with fingers spread. How old is it? Please tell me. The girl holds out both hands, and spreads her fingers. She tries to understand, fails, and stays there with her two hands outstretched. Ten months, she must mean. The lady goes away again, shouting something. She gathers up the child and the cloth, and carries them indoors.

In the garden, in the quiet of the afternoon, the girl falls asleep.

She wakes: the lady is back. There is something else she wants to know. The girl answers: 'Battambang.' The lady leaves her. The girl dozes off again. She is no longer leaning against the tree. She is stretched out full length in the drive. Clutched in her hand is the piastre she was given this morning. The lady has not bothered her again, but the girl still does not quite trust her. Battambang will keep her safe. She will never utter any word but that. It is her shelter, her home. But why, if she still mistrusts her, does she not go? Because she needs rest? No, not exactly. She does not want to leave this place yet, not as long as she has no notion of where to go from here, or what to do next.

In the course of the afternoon, the problem resolves itself. How can she even consider turning back, after what she has done?

She wakes. It is night. The verandah is brightly lit: the lady is bending over the child again. Now, she is alone with it. Will she make another attempt to wake it? No, it's

something else. The girl hitches herself up to see. The lady lays the child on the table, goes away, and comes back with a bowl of water. She picks up the child again and, talking softly to it as she does so, immerses it in the water. She is no longer angry with them, emaciated children that they are, because she can see that the baby is, after all, alive. Why else should she be bathing it? Would she be giving a bath to a dead child? She, the child's mother, knew all along. Now the lady knows too. Two people know. It is peaceful here in the garden. No doubt her presence here, under the trees, is almost forgotten. Things have been happening. There is a big bowl of cooling soup at her feet, resting against a tree. They must have brought it while she was asleep, and they did not wake her with kicks. Next to the soup is a bottle of lotion for her injured foot.

She eats, and as she eats, she watches the lady rub the child with the palm of her hand, talking to it all the while. The little head is covered with white suds. The girl laughs to herself without making a sound. The girl scrambles to her feet. She goes a few steps nearer, to watch. This is the first time she has ventured to move since this morning. She is careful to keep out of sight. The lady must not see her. Never again. She sees that the baby is asleep in the water. The white lady is not talking now. She is drying the child with the white cloth. The girl draws nearer still. The child's eyelids flicker. She gives a little cry, and then falls asleep again, wrapped in the cloth. From where she is standing, the girl can see clearly, but she retreats into the shadows, and goes back to her tree. It is very dark under the dense foliage of the custard-apple tree. She sits in the shadow of the tree to avoid being seen, and once more settles down to wait.

The footpaths will be clearly visible in the light of the full moon. She picks up one of the windfall custard-apples and

tastes it, a sugary white paste, sickly, deceptively like milk. No. She puts the custard-apple back on the ground.

She is not hungry.

The outlines of buildings and their shadows are sharply defined. The forecourt is deserted, the roads too, no doubt. The gate is probably locked, but it should not be too difficult to scramble through the hedge.

A bell rings. A servant comes to the gate to answer it. A white man, carrying an attaché case, appears. The gate shuts behind him. The servant and the white man go past the girl, but do not notice her. The white man is with the lady. They talk. The lady unwraps the child, shows it to the man, and then wraps it up again. They go into the house together, leaving the verandah lights on. All is quiet again.

Song of Battambang, sometimes I used to fall asleep on the back of the great buffalo, replete with the hot rice my mother gave me. The mother, thin and furious, reduces her memory to ashes with one searing blow.

It is not possible to sing here in this garden. On the other side of the wall, beyond the hibiscus hedge, there is the open road, leading everywhere. Here, the house. There, an evenly spaced row of other buildings, a door, three windows, a door, three windows. A school. It must be a school. There was a school in Battambang. Was there a school in Battambang? She has forgotten. In front of her, behind the buildings, are locked gates, a wall, a hibiscus hedge. Here, next to the bowl of soup, on the ground, a bandage, and the little bottle of greyish liquid. The girl squeezes her foot, squeezes out the pus, pours the greyish liquid on the wound, and bandages her foot. Some months before, at a medical centre, they treated her foot in this way. Her foot is like lead, especially after stopping for a while, but she feels no pain. She gets up, and looks at the gate and the door. She can hear voices inside the house. Home to Battambang, home to

that emaciated woman, her mother. She beats her children. They scramble up the slopes to get away from her. She shouts. She calls them in for their meal of hot rice. Her eyes water in the smoke-filled hut. To have one last glimpse of her, to be a child again for the last time, before setting out again, perhaps to die. To see her angry just once more.

She will never find her way home. She will no longer want to.

A breeze stirs the trees and causes the shadows to flicker. The roads leading to Tonle Sap are carpeted with velvet. She looks about her, rotates—how to get out of here?—scratches her breasts, itching because of the few drops of milk that even now collect there at night. She is not hungry. She stretches. Oh! what it is to be young, to run, to walk at night, singing the songs of Tonle Sap. All of them. Ten years later, in Calcutta, there will be only one song. It will be the last remnant of memory left to her.

Ever since the arrival of the white man, there has been light in one of the windows. That is where the voices are coming from. Once more she tiptoes nearer—but this time meaning to be on her way—and hitches herself up on to the coping that surrounds the house. They are still there, the two of them, the two whites. Stretched out on the lap of an angry mother, her child lies asleep. The mother is no longer looking at it. Nor is the white man. He is standing with a syringe in his hand. There is the milk-bottle, still full, on a table. The lady is no longer shrieking. The lady is crying. What floods of tears! The child from which she has parted opens its eyes and drops off to sleep again, it half-opens its eyes, and drops off again, over and over, endlessly. It no longer concerns me. It is the business of other women now. You in addition to myself, an impossible association, yet how hard it was to separate us, the round head protruded from the sack behind me, and rolled from side to side whenever

I skipped or stumbled. I should have gone slowly and carefully, but I ran. I should have kept my eyes on the ground, watching out for large stones, but I walked with my head in the air, and often tripped over the stones. The doctor approaches the newly-washed infant, and gives it an injection. The child gives a feeble cry. The girl is not unfamiliar with this kind of healing. She has seen injections being given in medical centres. Unconsciously, she mimics the grimace on the child's crumpled face. For the rest of her life she will feel, between her shoulders, the pressure of the child's weight, her exact weight now. Alive or dead, for her the child will never exceed that weight. The girl leaves the spot from which she has been watching. She turns her back, now bare of its burden, on the window. She leaves. She scrambles through the hibiscus hedge. She finds herself back in one of the streets of the white township.

Well-fed as she is tonight, she longs to talk to someone in the language of Battambang. She longs to see again that woman, the unkindest she has ever known. If she cannot, what is to become of her? Who? She takes a few steps. With aching back, and stabbing pains in her belly, she walks, she goes on. Aloud, she speaks a few words of Cambodian: Good morning, Good night. She used to talk to the child. To whom is she talking now? To her old mother in the Plain of Tonle Sap, the fountain-head, the instigator of all her misfortunes, her blighted destiny, her innocent love. She fights against the stabbing pains of colic, and walks on a few steps. Suffocating nausea, from her overloaded stomach, rises in her throat. She longs to bring up the food, to breathe. She stops and turns round. A gate opens. It is the same gate. The same white man comes out through it. She thought she had left the house far behind. She is no longer afraid of the white man. He walks hurriedly past, without seeing her.

The lights go out in the house.

It can only be a day or two since the end of the full monsoon, with its rainfall beyond measure, day after day, days without number.

How late she will be getting back to her mother, how late getting home. Home, in the north, where children play, where there are people with whom she can laugh and exchange greetings. Home, where she is going, to be beaten by her mother, to be beaten to death. She takes the piastre from between her breasts, and examines it by the light of the moon.

She will not return it. She drops it back into her bodice, and then starts to go forward. Yes, this time she really does go forward.

She has escaped through the hibiscus hedge, she is sure of that. She has left.

A quay: the Mekong River. Black junks moored to the banks. They will sail in the night. Since Battambang is beyond her reach, she adopts this village as her own. There are young people playing mandolins. Among the junks, a soup vendor plies his wares in a little boat; further off there are two more little boats lit by kerosene lamps; pots of soup are simmering over fires on the decks. Singing can be heard from under the canvas awning of a boat close inshore. She begins walking the length of the junks moored end to end, with the heavy, even tread of a peasant. She, too, is moving out tonight.

She will never again return to the north, writes Peter Morgan. She will follow the Mekong River upstream, meaning to travel north, but one morning she will turn back.

She will follow one tributary of the Mekong after another.

One night, she will find herself in a forest.

Another night, she will come to a river. She will follow this river too. It is a very long river. She wanders away from it. Another forest. She sets off again. Rivers. Roads. She passes through Mandalay, follows the Irrawaddy downstream, goes through Prome and Bassein, and comes to the Bay of Bengal.

One day she finds herself sitting on the ground, facing the sea.

She sets off again.

She reaches the north by way of the plains stretching away from the Chittagong and Arakan mountains.

One day, having been ten years on the way, she arrives in Calcutta.

She stays.

At the start, when she still had the freshness of youth, she was sometimes taken on board a junk. But the stench of her infected foot got steadily worse, and for weeks and months on end no one would take her. At this time, on account of her foot, men rarely wanted her. From time to time, however, there were men, foresters. Somewhere up in the mountains, she got treatment for her foot. She stayed for ten days or so in the forecourt of a medical centre. In spite of being

fed and cared for, she ran away from there too. When the foot heals, things will be better. Later there was the forest. Madness in the forest. She always sleeps close to a village. But sometimes there are no villages, and then she sleeps in a gravel pit or under a tree. She dreams: she is her dead child, or a buffalo in the rice-field. Sometimes she is the rice-field itself, or a forest. She who, night after night, will swim in the poisonous waters of the Ganges and survive, dreams that she too is dead, drowned.

Many things combine to strip her of the last vestiges of sanity: hunger in Pursat, and other places since, of course, but also the sun, the lack of anyone to talk to, the oppressive buzzing of insects in the forest, the stillness of the clearings. She grows more and more confused, until at last, suddenly, all confusion ceases, because she no longer seeks to understand anything. What does she get to eat on this long, long journey? A little rice on the outskirts of a village, and sometimes, yes, the carcases of birds killed by tigers and left lying on the ground to ripen, fruit and fish. She learnt to hunt for fish before she ever saw the Ganges.

How many children were born to her on the way? By the time she got to Calcutta, with its abundance of food in the overflowing dustbins of the Prince of Wales Hotel, and hot rice whenever she wanted it at a little garden gate she knew, she was sterile.

Calcutta.

She stays.

It is ten years since she left home.

Peter Morgan has stopped writing.

It is one o'clock in the morning. Peter Morgan goes out. Calcutta at night smells of stagnant water and saffron.

She is not there on the river bank. There is no one under her bush. Peter Morgan goes to look for her in the yard behind the Embassy kitchens. She is not there either. She is not swimming in the Ganges. He knows that she sometimes goes to the Islands, travelling on the roofs of buses, lured there during the summer monsoon by the garbage bins of the Prince of Wales Hotel. They are there, the lepers, fast asleep.

Peter Morgan heard from Anne-Marie Stretter the story of a mother who sold her child. It occurred seventeen years ago, somewhere near Savannakhet in Laos. Anne-Marie Stretter was present. The beggar-woman, Anne-Marie Stretter believes, speaks the language of Savannakhet. The dates do not coincide. The beggar-woman is too young to be the one Anne-Marie Stretter saw. Nevertheless, Peter Morgan has woven Anne-Marie Stretter's story into his account of the life of the beggar-woman.

Anne-Marie Stretter's little girls say that the beggar-woman stands under their balcony for hours, smiling up at them.

Peter Morgan is forced to resort to fragments stored in his own memory, to fill in the blanks in the beggar-woman's forgotten past. Otherwise, Peter Morgan would be at a loss to explain the madness of the beggar-woman of Calcutta.

Calcutta. She stays. It is ten years since she left home. How long since she lost her memory? How to put into words the things she never said? How to say what she will not say? How to describe the things that she does not know she has seen, the experiences that she does not know she has had? How to reconstruct the forgotten years?

Peter Morgan walks through the sleeping city. He walks beside the Ganges. Passing the European Club, he sees two shadowy figures on the terrace, the Vice-Consul and the Club Secretary. They are there every night, those two, talking.

Just now, it is the Vice-Consul who is speaking. There is no mistaking that wheezing voice. From where he is, Peter Morgan can hear almost nothing of what they are saying, but, instead of venturing nearer, Peter Morgan retreats. He does not wish to hear so much as a word of the Vice-Consul's confidences.

Peter Morgan walks back towards the Embassy, and is lost from sight in the grounds.

There is only one bridge four in the Club tonight. Most people are having an early night, in anticipation of the reception tomorrow. The Club Secretary and the Vice-Consul are sitting side by side on the terrace, looking out over the Ganges. These two do not play cards, they talk. The bridge-players in the card-room cannot overhear their conversation.

'I've been here twenty years,' the Secretary is saying. 'The things I've seen and heard. . . . If only I could write, what a novel they would make!'

The Vice-Consul, his eyes fixed on the Ganges, as usual does not reply.

'There's a magic about countries like this,' the Secretary goes on. 'Unforgettable! One could never settle down in Europe again. This eternal summer . . . trying, of course . . . but one gets used to the heat . . . oh! the heat . . . when one is back there, remembering the heat . . . the endless summer. . . . What a fantastic climate!'

'A fantastic climate!' echoes the Vice-Consul.

Every night, the Club Secretary talks about India, and tells the Vice-Consul the story of his life. Then the Vice-Consul of France in Lahore tells the Secretary as much of his life story as he thinks fit. The Club Secretary knows how to handle the Vice-Consul: with a trickle of boring facts, to which the Vice-Consul does not listen, he occasionally succeeds in provoking him at last into saying something. Sometimes the Vice-Consul, in his wheezing voice, talks

incoherently and at great length. At other times, he is perfectly lucid. To all appearances, the Vice-Consul is unaware of the fact that every word he says is repeated to the whole of Calcutta. He is unaware of it. No one except the Club Secretary ever addresses a word to him.

The Club Secretary is often questioned about what the Vice-Consul has been saying to him. Everyone in Calcutta wants to know.

The bridge-players have gone. The Club is deserted. The lights, tiny bulbs strung like a necklace along the terrace, have been turned off. The Vice-Consul has been subjecting the Club Secretary to a long inquisition on the subject of Anne-Marie Stretter, her lovers, her marriage, her interests, her trips to the Islands. But even after he has, apparently, found out all he wanted to know, he does not seem ready to leave. They are both silent now. They have been drinking. They drink heavily every night on the Club terrace. The Secretary hopes to end his days in Calcutta, never to return to Europe. He has told the Vice-Consul of his wish, and the Vice-Consul has assured him that, as far as he concerned, he is welcome to stay.

Tonight, although the Vice-Consul has questioned the Club Secretary closely on the subject of Anne-Marie Stretter, he himself has said very little. Every night, the Secretary hopes he will reveal more about himself. And tonight, he does.

The Vice-Consul asks:

'Do you think it is ever possible to be successful in love, if one doesn't make an effort to help things along?'

The Secretary has no idea what the Vice-Consul is talking about.

'Do you think it necessary to give love a helping hand before it will declare itself, or precipitate matters so that one morning one may wake up to find oneself in love?'

The Secretary still does not understand.

57

'One fixes upon an object,' the Vice-Consul goes on. 'One sets it up, in a manner of speaking, before one's eyes, and one bestows one's love upon it. A woman would be the simplest choice.'

The Secretary asks the Vice-Consul if he is in love with some woman in Calcutta. The Vice-Consul disregards this question.

'A woman would be the simplest choice,' reiterates the Vice-Consul. 'It's something I have only just discovered. Have I ever told you, I have never been in love?'

This is the first the Secretary has heard of it. He yawns, but the Vice-Consul takes no notice.

'I am a virgin,' the Vice-Consul goes on.

The Secretary, shaken out of his alcoholic stupor, stares at the Vice-Consul.

'I have made several attempts to fall in love with various persons, but I have never been able to see it though to the end. You might say that my life has been one long effort to experience love, if you see what I mean, Mr. Secretary.'

The Secretary has a notion that he does not understand what the Vice-Consul is talking about. He says, 'I'm listening.' He waits expectantly.

'For the past few weeks,' the Vice-Consul continues, 'I have felt that the effort was no longer necessary.'

The Vice-Consul turns to face the Club Secretary. He points to himself.

'Take a good look at my face,' he says.

The Secretary looks away. The Vice-Consul goes back to staring at the Ganges.

'Having failed to find an object for my love, I attempted to find consolation in self-love, but I failed in that too. All the same, until recently, I have always preferred my own company to that of other people.'

'I don't think you know what you're saying.'

'You may be right,' says the Vice-Consul. 'The years I have devoted to the pursuit of self-love have crippled me.'

'I really believe you are a virgin,' says the Secretary.

He appears to derive some satisfaction from this admission.

'Everyone here will be relieved to hear it,' the Secretary goes on.

'Look into my face and describe what you see, Mr. Secretary,' orders the Vice-Consul.

'Impossible!' replies the Secretary.

Impassively, the Vice-Consul pursues his train of thought:

'The day I arrived here,' he says, 'I saw a woman in the Embassy gardens, going towards the tennis courts. It was early in the morning. I was walking in the grounds when I met her.'

'It must have been Madame Stretter herself!' exclaims the Secretary.

'Possibly,' says the Vice-Consul.

'Younger than her husband. Beautiful still?'

'Possibly.'

He falls silent.

'Did she see you?' asks the Secretary.

'Yes.'

'Can you tell me anything more?'

'Such as what?'

'This meeting. . . .'

'This meeting? . . .' echoes the Vice-Consul.

'The effect of this meeting on you. Can you tell me about that?'

The Vice-Consul gives the matter some thought.

'What do you think, Mr. Secretary? Do you think there's anything I can tell you about it?'

The Secretary gapes at him.

'Whatever you tell me, you may be sure that it will be just between the two of us. I promise you that.'

59

'I'm trying to think,' says the Vice-Consul.

Silence falls between them once more. The Secretary yawns. The Vice-Consul does not seem to notice.

'Well?' asks the Secretary.

'I can only repeat what I have already told you: on the day I arrived here, I saw a woman in the Embassy grounds. She was going towards the deserted tennis courts. It was early in the morning. I happened to be walking in the grounds at the same time, and we met. Do you want me to go on?'

'This time,' says the Secretary, 'you mentioned that the tennis courts were deserted.'

'That is not without significance,' says the Vice-Consul. 'The tennis courts were, in fact, deserted.'

'Did that really make any difference?'

The Secretary sniggers.

'A very great difference indeed,' replies the Vice-Consul.

'In what way?'

'In creating an atmosphere, perhaps? Why not?'

The Vice-Consul does not expect any reply from the Club Secretary. The Secretary does not turn a hair. In his opinion, the Vice-Consul is subject to fits of delirium. The only thing to do, when the Vice-Consul lapses into incoherence, is to wait for the fit to pass.

'Mr. Secretary,' pursues the Vice-Consul, 'you have not answered my question.'

'It did not call for an answer, sir. You did not expect any. No one could answer it. The tennis courts . . . go on, I'm listening.'

'It was not until after she had left that I realized they were deserted. I heard a tearing sound. She had caught her skirt on a bush. And her eyes were looking into mine.'

The Vice-Consul slumps forward, as the Secretary continues to gape at him. The Vice-Consul often sits like this, motionless, with his head sunk on his chest.

'There was a bicycle there, up against the wire netting round the tennis courts. She mounted it, and rode off down the drive,' the Vice-Consul continues.

In spite of all his efforts, the Secretary cannot read the expression on the Vice-Consul's face. Here again, the Vice-Consul's remarks do not call for any reply.

'How does a woman go about things?' asks the Vice-Consul.

The Secretary guffaws.

'Well, really!' he protests, 'you're drunk.'

'I've heard people say that she seems very sad at times. Is that true, Mr. Secretary?'

'Yes.'

'Is that what her lovers say?'

'Yes.'

'I should play on her sadness,' says the Vice-Consul, 'if I got the chance.'

'And if not?'

'I might find a way of approaching her through something she had touched . . . the bush . . . or the bicycle, perhaps. Are you awake, Mr. Secretary?'

The Vice-Consul, brooding, forgets the Secretary for a time. Then he says:

'Mr. Secretary, please don't fall asleep.'

'I'm not asleep,' mumbles the Secretary.

Tonight, the dining-room was empty except for two English-men passing through Calcutta. They have now left.

The reception at the Embassy is due to start in about two hours' time, at eleven. The Club is deserted. The lights are out in the bar. The Secretary is sitting on the terrace over-looking the Ganges. He is waiting for the Vice-Consul tonight as usual.

Here he comes. He sits, like the Secretary, facing the Ganges. They drink for a time in silence.

'Listen to me, Mr. Secretary,' the Vice-Consul at length says.

Tonight, the Secretary has had even more to drink than last night.

'I was sitting here waiting,' says the Secretary, 'though I don't exactly know what for. Maybe it was you, sir?'

'Me,' the Vice-Consul agrees.

'I'm listening.'

The Vice-Consul does not speak. The Secretary takes him by the arm and shakes him.

'Tell me some more about the deserted tennis courts,' says the Secretary.

'The bicycle is still there. It hasn't been moved since that woman left it there twenty-three days ago.'

'Forgotten?'

'No.'

'You're wrong there, sir,' says the Secretary. 'The mon-soon has stopped her from riding it in the grounds, and she's forgotten about it.'

62

'No. That's not so,' says the Vice-Consul.

The Vice-Consul is silent for so long that the Secretary almost drops off to sleep. The Vice-Consul's wheezing voice rouses him.

'At boarding school in Seine-et-Oise, I learnt for the first time what it was to have fun,' he says. 'Have I ever told you about it?'

Not yet. The Secretary yawns, but the Vice-Consul pays no attention.

'All right, you had fun. So what?' says the Secretary.

'Having fun. I discovered what that meant at Montfort Secondary School in Seine-et-Oise. Are you listening, Mr. Secretary?'

The Club Secretary says, 'I am listening.' He is prepared to listen.

In his wheezing voice the Vice-Consul unburdens himself to the Secretary, who dozes off, wakes up with a start, sniggers, dozes off, and wakes again. But the Vice-Consul does not seem in the least put off by his companion's obvious boredom. The Vice-Consul describes the fun he had at Montfort.

The fun at Montfort, the Vice-Consul explains, consisted in breaking up the place. It was something a lot of them wanted to do. As to the means of achieving this object, the Vice-Consul says, he knows of none better than those employed at Montfort. Stink bombs, at meal times to begin with, then in the teachers' studies, then in the class-rooms, then in the common room and the dormitories, then . . . then. . . . There was an enormous amount of laughter, they were doubled up with laughter at Montfort Secondary School.

'Stink bombs, fake turds, fake slugs, fake mice,' pursues the Vice-Consul. 'Real turds everywhere, on all the masters' desks. We were a filthy lot at Montfort.'

63

He stops. The Secretary is unmoved. The Vice-Consul is raving again tonight. A bad attack, this.

'The headmaster used to say,' the Vice-Consul resumes, 'that in all his nineteen years as a schoolteacher, he had never seen anything like it. To quote his exact words: "Persistent and infamous delinquency." He promised remission of punishment to any informer. There was none, not one in the whole school. Never. There were thirty-two of us, and not a single defection. Our conduct in the classroom was exemplary. We were no longer mischievous for mischief's sake. We pinpointed our target, concentrated our attack, and struck harder day by day. The whole school was pressed into service. Day by day we were learning how to make things worse for them. Everyone was waiting for the final explosion. Do you understand?'

The Club Secretary stirs in his sleep.

'What a bore!' he says.

The Vice-Consul shakes him awake.

'I'm sure all that I've been telling you is just what everybody wants to hear. Don't drop off again! Your turn, Mr. Secretary.'

'What do you want to know, sir?'

'I want a quid pro quo, Mr. Secretary.'

'In our case,' began the Secretary, 'in my case, it was a corrective training establishment right in the country, near Arras in the Pas-de-Calais. There were four hundred and seventy-two of us. They had fellows sneaking about the dormitories at night, trying to catch us out, but we got the better of them all. Don't you go dropping off, either! One morning, our science master stalked into the classroom, and announced that as we should shortly be having tests—as I recall—keep awake, if you don't mind—the lesson would be devoted to revising deserts, sandhills, beaches, porous rock-formations, aquatic plants and also, he said, the botanic

64

group known—so felicitously, he remarked—as plants of light and shade. Today, therefore, said the science master, we would revise. What a splendid lot of boys we were! You could have heard a pin drop. . . . "What's that nasty smell?" says the master. "There really is a nasty smell. I don't mean it metaphorically." Don't fall asleep. This was it! The master opened a drawer to get out a stick of chalk; he found a turd. Thinking it was just another plaster cast, such as he found there the day before, he picked it up and crushed it in his hand. You should have heard him yell! . . . and yell! . . .'

'And then, you see, Mr. Secretary. . . .'

'What?'

'Carry on, Mr. Secretary.'

'Then all the masters came pouring into the classroom, and the headmaster, too, and all the assistants and the servants. There were we doubled up with laughter, and there were they gaping at us, speechless, unable to find a word to say to us. I forgot to mention that the science master was holding up his right hand, while holding in his left hand a note that I had written and put in the drawer with the excrement. It read: "Prisoner at the bar, raise your right hand full of excrement and say: I swear that I am an idiot." The headmaster came in again in the afternoon. He was white as a sheet. I can still hear his voice: "Who excreted in the drawers?" He went on to say that he was in possession of certain evidence. The excrement had spoken.'

The Vice-Consul of France and the Club Secretary can barely see one another in the dark. The Secretary sniggers.

'I dare say it was fun for you too, Mr. Secretary?'

'As you say, sir.'

'Very well then, Mr. Secretary, go on.'

'After that, our field of action was restricted, but we still found opportunities for mischief. We gagged the cook and

locked him in the kitchens. We tripped people in the aisle as they were going up to the altar for Holy Communion. We double-locked all the school doors, and smashed every light bulb in the place.'

'How did it end? In expulsion?'

'Yes. No more school for me. What about you, sir?'

'Expulsion. I lived in hopes of being sent to another boarding school, but no one did anything about it. All the same, I was able to attain a higher level of education than yours. I lived alone with my mother. She was grieving over the defection of her lover.'

'The Hungarian doctor?'

'Exactly. My mother is an adulteress. I, too, mourn. I miss her lover, who used to joke and play tricks in the common room at Montfort.'

'They are most anxious to know more of your childhood, sir.'

'I'm doing my best.'

'I can never be sure you're not leading me up the garden path, sir. Oh, well, no matter. What happened to you after your mother married the recording engineer from Brest?'

'I am in my house in Neuilly. A long time has passed since my departure from Montfort, and the death, yes, the death of my dead father. Did I tell you? My father died six months after my expulsion from Montfort. Dry-eyed, with arms folded, I watch him being lowered into his grave. I am, as you might expect, the cynosure of all eyes, notably the tear-dimmed eyes of the staff of a bank in Neuilly.'

'What did you do, sir, all on your own in Neuilly?'

'The same thing as you were doing elsewhere, Mr. Secretary.'

'And what might that be?'

'I attend surprise parties, where I haven't a word to say for myself. I am pointed out: "He drove his father into his

grave." I dance. My deportment is correct. To put it in a nutshell, Mr. Secretary, I am waiting for India, waiting for you, though I do not yet know it. In the meantime, in Neuilly, I am clumsy. I smash electric light bulbs. Better say the bulbs fell to the ground with a crash. I can hear the din in the empty passages. I authorize you to say: "Even as long ago as that, in Neuilly, if you see what I mean." Say: "He was frozen with horror. A young man alone in an empty house, smashing light bulbs, asking himself why? why?" Don't tell the whole story all at once. Spin it out.'

'What you are hiding, sir?'

'Nothing, Mr. Secretary.'

The Vice-Consul's eyes are truthful.

'Mr. Secretary,' pursues the Vice-Consul, 'I should like to prolong this period of my life, here in Calcutta. I am not waiting impatiently for my posting to come through, as may be generally believed. On the contrary, I hope it will be put off and put off, if possible until the end of the monsoon.'

'Because of her?' the Secretary asks with a smile.

'Mr. Secretary, you have my permission to repeat all I have told you to anyone who cares to listen. The more they know about me, the better my chances of staying a little longer in Calcutta. Does that satisfy you for tonight, Mr. Secretary?'

'Well,' says the Secretary, 'I dare say it will have to do. May I mention the deserted tennis courts as well?'

'Everything, Mr. Secretary, everything.'

The Vice-Consul once more requests the Club Secretary to tell him about the Islands, in particular the one to which she often goes, yes, once more. This is the time of the year, says the Secretary, when the cyclones build up, causing increasingly heavy seas. At night, the palm trees writhe in the wind. The island where she goes is the largest. There the wind tears through like a whistling train. The palm trees

67

moan, sounding like express trains roaring through the country-side. The palm grove of the Prince of Wales Hotel is world-famous. At its northern end, it is protected from vandals by an electric fence, and a good thing too. The landing stage is fringed with mango trees, and the grounds wooded with eucalyptus. It is the custom in India to surround luxury hotels with palm trees. The sky over the Indian Ocean is red at sunset, more often than not, and everywhere on the island the footpaths are striped with long dark shadows in the reddish light, shadows cast by the trunks of the palm trees. There are palm groves all over India, in the Malabar region, in Ceylon. The palm grove of the Prince of Wales is intersected by a broad avenue leading to the little private bungalows, which are part of the discreet and luxurious service offered by the hotel. Ah! the Prince of Wales! On the western shore of the island is a lagoon, but no one ever goes there, because, if the Club Secretary remembers rightly, it is outside the perimeter of the hotel grounds. Well, that's it.

The Secretary asks the Vice-Consul if he is going to the reception tonight.

Yes, he is. In fact, he is going now. He gets up. The Secretary looks at him earnestly.

'I shan't mention the tennis courts to anyone,' says the Secretary. 'Even if you ask me to.'

'It's up to you.'

He walks away across the Club lawn. The Secretary watches him in the yellowish light of the standard lamps. He sways slightly as he walks. He is too tall, too thin. He disappears into Victoria Avenue.

The Secretary returns to his seat facing the Ganges.

He reflects that, in future, their evenings together will be more boring than ever, because it seems as though the Vice-Consul of France in Lahore is left with virtually nothing

more to tell or invent about his life. The Club Secretary, too, is left with virtually nothing more to tell or invent about his own life, the Islands, or the wife of the French Ambassador in Calcutta.

The Secretary drops off to sleep.

A window lights up in one of the houses overlooking the avenue that runs beside the Ganges. It is the Vice-Consul's.

For any passer-by to see, he is there, wearing his dinner-jacket, prowling from room to room under the rotating electric fans. Seen from across the avenue, his expression would appear serene.

He goes out. There he is, crossing the grounds, making for the lighted windows of the reception rooms in the French Embassy.

Tonight, in Calcutta, the Ambassador's wife, Anne-Marie Stretter, is standing near the buffet. She is smiling. She is wearing black. Her dress has a double overskirt of black tulle. She is handing someone a glass of champagne. Having got rid of it, she looks about her. She has grown thin with the years, and now, on the threshold of old age, the refinement of her features and her tall bony figure show to advantage. Her eyes, too light for her colouring, are sculpted like the eyes of a statue, and her eyelids are transparent.

She looks about her. Her expression, that of an exile, is the same as she wears when, standing on the official rostrum in a square named after a conqueror, she watches a detachment of the Foreign Legion march past in the sunshine, singing, glittering in their red forage caps.

Among all those present, one man only notices it, Charles Rossett, aged thirty-two, who has been in Calcutta just three weeks, having come to take up his post as First Secretary.

She goes up to a group of English guests, and urges them to ask at the buffet for whatever refreshments they want. They are served by barmen in turbans.

People are saying: 'Do you see? She's invited the Vice-Consul of Lahore.'

It is quite a large gathering. There are, in all, about forty people in the room. The reception rooms are vast, like those of a casino in a summer resort outside Paris. The only differences are the huge, whirring electric fans, and the fine wire netting over the windows, through which the gardens

can be seen as through a mist. No one is looking out. The ballroom is octagonal, with walls of green marble in Empire taste. In each corner of the octagon is an arrangement of delicate ferns, ordered from France. On one wall hangs a portrait of a President of the Republic and, next to it, one of a Foreign Minister. People are saying: 'At the very last minute, she invited the Vice-Consul of Lahore.'

Now she is opening the ball with the Ambassador, performing the despised ritual, so that the other couples can take their place on the dance floor.

The ceiling fans make a sound like a flock of startled birds beating their wings, hovering above the couples dancing to the music of a slow foxtrot, above the cheap chandeliers, the hollowness, the sham, the gold paint. People are saying: 'That's him, that dark man near the bar. Whatever can have made her ask him?'

There is an aura of intriguing mystery about this woman of Calcutta. No one is quite sure what she does with her time. She seldom entertains, especially here in her official residence overlooking the Ganges, which dates back to the time of the East India Company. Nevertheless, it is presumed that she must do something. Was it only after eliminating every other possible alternative that it was decided that she was a great reader? Yes. What else could she be doing, shut up in her private apartments, during the hours between tennis and her evening drive. Crates of books, addressed to her, have been known to arrive from France. What else? Apparently, she spends a large part of her day with her daughters, who look like her. It is known that they have a young English governess, and generally believed that they lead a full and happy life, and that Anne-Marie Stretter takes a great personal interest in their up-bringing. Occasionally, when there is a reception, they put in a brief appearance, as they have already done this evening. Already they are a little aloof,

which, it is suspected, does not displease their mother. After they have left, murmured comments can be heard: Undoubtedly, the elder will be a beauty, like her mother, she has all her charm already. You can see all three of them there any morning, in white shorts, in the Embassy grounds, and every morning they either play tennis or go for a walk.

Someone asks: 'But what exactly did he do? I'm quite in the dark.'

'He did the very worst thing. How can I put it?'

'The very worst thing? Did he kill someone?'

'He fired shots in the Shalimar Gardens, where lepers and dogs shelter at night.'

'Lepers and dogs! Can you call it killing, when it's merely a question of lepers and dogs?'

'There was something else too. The mirrors of his residence in Lahore were riddled with bullets, you know.'

'You may have noticed that, from a distance, a leper looks much like anyone else, which suggests. . . .'

For some time following her arrival in Calcutta, no one knew of the now famous villa at one of the salubrious island resorts in the Ganges Delta. The villa belongs to the French Embassy, and is at the disposal of members of the staff. It was only when Anne-Marie Stretter's daughters were seen walking alone in the gardens that people began asking where their mother was, and were told that she was at the villa. The girls are most often seen walking alone in the frightful heat of the summer monsoon.

'Can you hear shouting?'

'What is it? Lepers? Or dogs?'

'Dogs or lepers.'

'Why say dogs or lepers, when you know perfectly well which it is?'

'In the distance, with the music playing, it's hard to

distinguish between the dogs barking and the lepers crying out in their sleep.'

'That's one way of putting it.'

Every evening, the three of them, in an open car, drive through the streets of Calcutta. The Ambassador, smiling, watches his treasures go off in the car: his wife and daughters are going to Chandernagore or to the sea coast on this side of the Delta, to get a breath of fresh air.

Neither the little girls nor anyone in Calcutta knows what she does at the villa in the Delta. It is said that she has lovers, Englishmen, who do not move in diplomatic circles. It is said that the Ambassador knows. She never spends more than a day or two at a time at the villa in the Delta. On returning to Calcutta, she at once resumes her well-regulated life, tennis, drives in the car, an occasional evening at the European Club. So much, anyone can see. And the rest of the time? No one knows. All the same, she must occupy her time somehow, this woman of Calcutta.

People are saying:

'It's beyond words!'

People are wondering:

'Did he do those things because he had a blackout, or what? Did he lose all self-control?'

'You must see how difficult. . . . How can one put into words what he did in Lahore, what he did with himself in Lahore, if he himself didn't know what he was doing?'

'At night, he used to stand on the balcony and shout.'

'Has he ever done that here?'

'Never. And why not, I wonder? It's even more stifling here.'

It is a little past midnight. Anne-Marie Stretter goes up to the young attaché, Charles Rossett. Beside him stands the Vice-Consul of France in Lahore. She suggests that they should dance, that is, of course, if they would like to, and then

she moves away. The general impression is that it is Charles Rossett she is interested in. He seems just the right man for her to take with her to the Islands, when she goes there in two or three days' time. Someone remarks that she would not have to be much more sparing with her smiles to be downright rude. She has invited some of her personal friends to tonight's reception, but they will not put in an appearance until the very end.

Someone asks:

'What was he shouting?'

'Gibberish.'

'Surely there must have been some woman in Lahore? She should be able to shed some light on it.'

'There wasn't any woman. There never has been.'

'Can you be sure he hadn't got one tucked away in the Residency? No one ever sets foot inside the Residency in Lahore.'

'Did no one ever notice anything odd about him all the time he was in Lahore? A queer look? A flush? The one I can't help thinking about is the mother of the Vice-Consul in Lahore. I imagine her seated at a piano, playing classical pieces, like the heroine of a novel, playing the melodies of her youth, with him listening, listening altogether too much, or so it would seem.'

'All the same, I do think she might have spared us the embarrassment of his presence here.'

It is expected of every man invited to a reception at the Embassy that he should ask Anne-Marie Stretter to dance, even though she herself may not wish it.

In passing, she says something to her husband about someone in the room. Charles Rossett lowers his eyes. It is obvious. The Vice-Consul, too, has noticed. He has been examining one of the delicate ferns, and running his finger down its black stem. People are thinking: he has only just

74

seen the Ambassador, on whose goodwill his next posting depends. Charles Rossett recalls that he has waited weeks for a summons that never comes.

People are saying: 'It is very broadminded of Monsieur Stretter to have allowed such a thing, to have agreed to his being invited tonight. He's a good man. He is nearing his retirement. We shall miss him. Yes, he is a lot older than she is. Her father was a District Officer in some backwater near the frontier of Laos, in French Indo-China. That's where he found her. Yes, seventeen years ago. She had only been there a few weeks when Monsieur Stretter paid an official visit to the district. It was barely a week later that he left, taking her with him. Didn't you know?'

They are saying: 'How well he has kept his figure, the Vice-Consul. You would take him for a much younger man, but for his face. . . . One day his mother just walked out and left him. Everyone in Calcutta knows. He talked to the Club Secretary about his childhood home, and his room, smelling of blotting paper and india rubber. From his window, he could see the down-and-outs in the Bois de Boulogne, gentle, humble men, most of them. He talked about his father, who spent every night at home, but never addressed a word to his mother. It's a lot of nonsense. He talks an awful lot of nonsense.'

Someone asks:

'Does he ever talk about Lahore?'

'No.'

'Never.'

'About his life before he went to Lahore?'

'Yes. About his childhood in Arras. But maybe that is just so as to pull the wool over our eyes.'

Someone says: 'So he picked her up in Laos, in French Indo-China, did he?'

They see: an avenue, with the Mekong River on one side

and a forest on the other. It is somewhere near Savannakhet, in Laos. They see sentries, infantrymen, guarding her for him until he should come and take her away. There was talk, it seems, of sending her back to France. She never could get used to it there. People are saying: 'Even now, no one in Calcutta really knows whether she was living a life of shame or sunk in despair when he found her in Savannakhet. No, no one ever found out.'

Every now and then the Vice-Consul's face lights up with joy. Just for a second, every now and then, he seems crazy with happiness. Tonight, it is impossible to avoid him. Is that the reason? How strange he looks tonight. How pale he is, as though he were in the grip of some intense emotion, holding it in check, endlessly deferring the moment when he will have to give expression to it. Why?

People are saying: 'Every evening, he talks to the Club Secretary. And for that matter, the Secretary is the only man who ever talks to him. There was that corrective training school in Arras that he told him about. It makes you think. The north. November. Flies clustering round naked light bulbs, brown linoleum. Those sort of places are all alike. It's as though one had been there oneself. Denim overalls in the playground. The Pas-de-Calais was shrouded in reddish fog all winter, he said . . . as though one had been there oneself . . . poor kids. But maybe he's just trying to pull the wool over our eyes.'

'Tell me more about Madame Stretter.'

'Above reproach, good-hearted, though of course there is always the inevitable gossip. . . . And she's charitable. She does things that her predecessors never even thought of. If you look behind the Embassy kitchens, you'll see fresh water put out for the beggars. She never forgets. She sees to it herself every morning before her game of tennis.'

'Above reproach? Come now.'

'She is the soul of discretion. And, in Calcutta, that is tantamount to being above reproach.'

'But what of him? He's done us a lot of harm. I'd never set eyes on him until tonight, so tall and dark, well set-up you could almost say, if . . . and so young. . . . It's a shame. I can't quite see his eyes . . . his face gives nothing away. The Vice-Consul of Lahore is a bit of a death's head. Wouldn't you agree that he's a bit of a death's head?'

Most of the women have pale complexions, like the nuns of an enclosed order. They spend their lives in shuttered rooms, sheltering from the deadly rays of the sun. In India they do virtually nothing. They are rested. Tonight, exposed to view, transported from their homes to this outpost of France in India, they are happy.

'This is the last reception of the season. The monsoon has begun. Did you notice the sky this morning? That's how it will be every day for the next six months.'

'What should we do without the Islands? They must be looking beautiful tonight. Ah! they are what we shall miss most when we leave India.'

The men are saying:

'It's like being back in France. It's extraordinary, the effect it has on one, seeing all these women here, even those one wouldn't look at twice at home.'

A man points to Anne-Marie Stretter.

'I see her almost every morning, walking across the grounds to the tennis courts. They're a grand sight, a woman's legs, in this loathsome place. Don't you agree? Forget that man, the Vice-Consul of Lahore.'

Charles Rossett and others are watching him covertly. The Vice-Consul does not seem to notice. Does he never sense that people are looking at him? It's impossible to tell. He still has that radiant look, though for what reason no one

can guess. What vision, what inspiration, can have so trans-figured him?

This morning the bicycle was still there, leaning against the wire netting.

The Ambassador said to Charles Rossett: 'Have a word with him. You really should.' He does so.

'I don't seem able to settle down,' Charles Rossett says. 'I must admit, I can't seem to settle down here.'

An answering smile. A sudden mellowing of the features. He sways a little, as when he walks in the Embassy grounds.

'It's not easy, of course, but what exactly is your difficulty?'

'The heat, of course,' says Charles Rossett, 'but there's the monotony as well. The quality of the light, it seems to drain all the colour out of life. I can't see myself getting used to it, ever.'

'As bad as that?'

'That's to say. . . .'

'Yes?'

'I hadn't any very high hopes to start with,' Charles Rossett says, then recollecting himself: 'What about you? Was there any particular place you would have preferred to . . . this?'

The Vice-Consul purses his lips.

'None,' he says.

It was some time after he was out of sight of Charles Rossett, who, in his turn, had gone over to look at the bicycle, that the Vice-Consul had begun whistling that old tune 'Indiana's Song.' That was yesterday. And it was then that Charles Rossett, more frightened than ever before, had started walking very rapidly towards the administrative buildings.

Charles Rossett says that he arrived here feeling like a student on vacation, but that he seems to be ageing visibly

with every day that passes. They both laugh. Someone remarks: 'Did you see that? He and that other fellow are laughing together. It really is the limit, you know, his accepting the invitation. It's effrontery. And yet, to look at him, you wouldn't think he had it in him.'

An elderly Englishman comes into the room. He is tall and thin, with sharp eyes, like a bird, and skin withered by the sun. One of those who have been in India for a long time. One can always tell. They're a race apart, don't you think? With an expansive gesture, he leads them towards the bar.

'Do help yourselves. Everyone does. My name is George Crawn. I'm a friend of Anne-Marie's.'

The Vice-Consul gives a little start. George Crawn moves off, and the Vice-Consul gazes intently at the retreating figure of the Englishman. He does not seem to notice that he is being stared at, nor that, wherever he goes, people shrink back, leaving him standing in a little clearing. He says:

'A member of the inner circle. Exclusiveness, that's the secret of India.'

He laughs. Charles Rossett, with a beckoning gesture, moves closer to the bar. The Vice-Consul, with apparent reluctance, follows.

'Come now,' says Charles Rossett. 'Here, I can assure you. . . . What are you afraid of?'

The Vice-Consul, still smiling, looks round the octagonal ballroom.

The tune, 'Indiana's Song,' evokes the memory of that lonely, dark, abominable act.

'Nothing. No, I know I have nothing more to lose. . . . I'm just waiting for my posting, that's all. It will take time, of course. It isn't easy. . . . I find it more difficult than most to keep up appearances,' he laughs again, 'to look as though I were up to the job, that's all.'

The Vice-Consul laughs. With head bent, he goes up to

the bar. Forget the woman's bicycle near the deserted tennis courts, or escape. It's not so much the look in his eyes, Charles Rossett reflects, as his voice. The Ambassador said to Charles Rossett: 'People avoid him instinctively; there's something frightening about the man . . . but the loneliness. . . . Do try and talk to him.'

'I understand that you have expressed a preference for Bombay.'

'Well, as they won't keep me in Calcutta, why not Bombay?'

'There aren't so many people in Bombay, the climate is better, and it's an advantage being so near the sea.'

'I dare say,' he looks up at Charles Rossett, 'you'll settle down here all right. You don't strike me as the kind who is accident-prone.'

Charles Rossett laughs. 'Thanks very much!' he says.

'I'm beginning to be able to tell those who are from those who are not,' the Vice-Consul goes on. 'You are not.'

Charles Rossett forces a laugh.

Anne-Marie Stretter goes past. The Vice-Consul of Lahore gazes after her.

Charles Rossett pays no particular attention to this. Assuming a bantering tone, he says: 'Your personal reports—if you'll forgive my mentioning it—describe you as an impossible person. Did you know that?'

'I have not asked for disclosure of the reports in my personal file, though I believe "unstable" was the word used. Was it not?'

'To be perfectly honest, I know very little. . . .' He is still keeping up the effort to smile. 'It's absurd. . . . What does "impossible" mean? Nothing at all!'

'What are they saying? What's the worst they've got against me?'

'Lahore.'

'Was what happened at Lahore really so shocking? Has nothing comparable ever happened before?'

'One can't avoid . . . forgive me for saying this, but one is baffled by the Lahore business. One doesn't know what to make of it.'

'That's true,' says the Vice-Consul.

He leaves Charles Rossett and takes up his former position near the door, beside a pedestal supporting a delicate potted fern. There he stands, the focus of all eyes.

But the sensation his presence created at the start is beginning to wear off.

She goes past again, almost brushing against him, but this time he does not look at her. It is very noticeable.

It is only then that Charles Rossett remembers that Madame Stretter used occasionally to take an early-morning bicycle ride in the Embassy grounds. She has not done so recently, but that is probably owing to the summer monsoon.

It is half-past twelve.

Under the overhanging bush on the banks of the Ganges, she wakes, stretches, and sees the big house ablaze with light: food. She gets up. She smiles. Instead of diving into the Ganges, she goes towards the lights. The other mad beggars of Calcutta are already there asleep, huddled together near the little back gate, waiting for the scraps to be distributed, much later, when the dishes have been cleared away.

There is a young woman standing alone in the octagonal ballroom, watching the dancers. On an impulse, the Vice-Consul goes up to her.

She accepts his invitation to dance in a flurried manner, which clearly reveals her embarrassment and agitation. They dance.

'Look over there, he's going to dance. He dances just like anyone else, very correctly.'

'It's best, really, to put it out of one's mind.'

'Quite. It's best to put it out of one's mind. But it isn't easy. And, come to think of it, why should one? What else is there to think about?'

Anne-Marie Stretter goes up to the buffet, where Charles Rossett is now standing alone. She gives him a friendly smile. He cannot avoid asking her to dance.

It is the first time. People are saying: 'This is the first time. Will she take a fancy to him?'

Charles Rossett and Anne-Marie Stretter have met before, about a fortnight ago. He was invited to an informal welcoming party in one of the elegantly furnished private rooms in the Embassy, where newcomers are always received. The Vice-Consul of France was invited then, as tonight. She was sitting on a couch upholstered in rose-coloured cretonne. He was startled by her expression, and her statuesque grace, as she sat on the couch.

The party lasted an hour. She did not move from the couch, where she sat, erect, in a white dress, with her daughters beside her. She was pale under her Calcutta tan, like all the other whites.

All three looked with interest at the two newcomers. Jean-Marc de H. said nothing. They asked Charles Rossett about himself, but did not address a word to the other man. Lahore was not mentioned, nor was he asked what he thought of Calcutta. The Vice-Consul was ignored. He was resigned to it. He stood there, not saying a word. It was the same with India. India, like the Vice-Consul, was ignored. At that time, Charles Rossett did not yet know of the Lahore scandal.

She told him she played tennis with her daughters, remarked that the swimming pool was delightful, and so on in this vein. It occurred to him that he would probably never see this little private room again, nor her. Would he ever see her again, except at official receptions and the European Club?

'How are you settling down in Calcutta?'

'Not too happily.'

'Forgive me, you are Charles Rossett, aren't you?'

'Yes.'

He smiled.

She raised her head and smiled back. It needed no more than one look for white society in Calcutta to open its doors to him.

She does not know, thinks Charles Rossett. He recalls that, as he stood there in silence, the Vice-Consul looked out of the window at the palm trees in the grounds, the oleanders, the wrought-iron gates in the distance, the sentries. Monsieur Stretter was talking about Peking to a visiting official. Did he know? With the Vice-Consul still standing there not uttering a word, she suddenly said: 'I wish I were in your place, seeing India for the first time, especially at this time of year, during the monsoon.'

They left sooner than they should have done.

She knows nothing. No one in Calcutta knows anything. Unless the Embassy gardeners saw something, but they will not talk. She must have forgotten that bicycle of hers, which she does not use during the summer monsoon.

As they dance, she says:

'I hope you're not bored here. What do you do with yourself in the evenings, and on Sunday?'

'I read. . . . I sleep. . . . I really don't know.'

'Well, you know, boredom is so much a matter of temperament, it's difficult to know what to suggest. . . .'

83

'I don't think I am bored.'

'I must thank you for the cases of books. You got them to me in record time. If it's books you want, just let me know, it's no trouble at all.'

In a flash, having captured her in flight, pinioned her, he sees her, as they dance, elsewhere, different: it is afternoon, her children are at their lessons, yes, she is trapped in the hollow of the siesta. He sees her in some secret corner of her residence, an unused servant's room, perhaps, curled up in a picturesque attitude, reading. No, he cannot see what she is reading. Reading, nights spent at the villa in the Delta, at first he sees these things in sharp focus, then they melt into the shadows, where things are said and done which it is impossible to imagine. What lies hidden in the shadow of Anne-Marie Stretter's luminous presence?

There is something alien about the gaiety of Anne-Marie Stretter, when she drives with her daughters along the road to Chandernagore in the torrid heat.

It is said that in that distant place, almost at the end of the Ganges, where she sleeps in a darkened room with her lover, she is subject to moods of profound melancholy. The whole thing is something of a mystery, but it is said that when she is in one of these moods, it is very restful to be with her, though what is meant by this, no one exactly knows.

'In spite of what you say,' Charles Rossett remarks, 'if I thought the past three weeks were a fair indication of what the next three years would be like, I don't think I could stand it.'

'Almost everything is impossible here, you know. I can't think of any other way of putting it, and yet it's just that that makes it so . . . extraordinary.'

'One day, perhaps. . . . Extraordinary? How do you mean?'

'No, it's . . . nothing. Living here is neither painful nor

pleasant, if you see what I mean. It's different, if you like. Contrary to popular belief, life here isn't easy, it isn't hard, it's nothing.'

At the Club, the other women talk about her. What does she do with herself? Where does she go? No one knows. She is at home in this nightmare town. Still waters run deep, they say. What really happened that time towards the end of her first year in Calcutta? No one ever discovered the reason for her sudden disappearance. The ambulance seen at dawn, parked at the Embassy gates. Attempted suicide? No one ever discovered the reason for her long absence in the mountains of Nepal. When she returned, she was so thin it was frightening. Was she changed in other ways? She is still very thin. That is all. It is said that it was not her love affair, her unhappy or all too happy love affair with Michael Richard that was at the back of it.

What would she say if she were to find out?

'I've heard it said that you are from Venice. Is it true? But then I've heard it said, too, at the Club, that it's not true.'

She laughs, and tells him that her mother is from Venice, yes.

He simply cannot imagine what she would say if she found out.

Anna Maria at eighteen, Anna Maria of the smiling eyes, painting in water-colours on one of the quays on the island of Giudecca. No, that's not right.

'My father was French. But I did live in Venice for a time, as a girl. We shall be going to Venice from here, or rather, that is our present intention.'

No, it must have been music for her in Venice, the piano. In Calcutta, she plays the piano almost every evening. Anyone walking in the avenue can hear her. It is generally agreed that, no matter what her origins, she must have

85

started learning music very young, at about the age of seven. Listening to her, one could well believe that music was her chief interest.

'The piano?'

'Yes, I've always had a piano, everywhere. I've played for years, more or less the whole time. . . .'

'I wondered where you came from. It might have been anywhere, I thought, between Ireland and Italy. I thought perhaps Dijon, Milan, Brest, Dublin, or somewhere in England. I thought you might be an Englishwoman.'

'And it didn't occur to you that I might be from somewhere more remote?'

'No, from anywhere more remote, you would not have been . . . you . . . here . . . in Calcutta.'

'Oh!' she says, smiling. 'You can never be sure, don't you see, with a woman of my age in Calcutta.'

'I wonder.'

'What I mean is, it's too simple to say that one comes from Venice, or only from Venice. It seems to me that one also comes from other places where one has stopped on the way.'

'Are you thinking of the French Vice-Consul?'

'Naturally, just as everyone else is. I'm told that they all want to know what kind of man he was before Lahore.'

'And, in your view, before Lahore there was nothing?'

'I believe that Lahore is where he comes from, yes.'

People are saying: 'Look at the Vice-Consul dancing. She, poor soul, couldn't refuse him. Since Anne-Marie Stretter has chosen to invite him, it would be an affront to her, who has foisted him on us.'

The Vice-Consul, dancing, has no eyes for his partner. He is watching Anne-Marie Stretter and Charles Rossett, who talk as they dance and, from time to time, exchange glances.

His dancing partner, the wife of the Spanish Consul, feels in duty bound to talk to the Vice-Consul of France in Lahore.

She remarks that she has seen him several times, in the Embassy grounds. It is such a small community, they are bound to meet sometimes. She has been here two and a half years, and will soon be leaving. The heat is very depressing. Some people never get used to it.

'Are there really people who never get used to it?' asks the Vice-Consul.

She draws away from him a little, but cannot yet bring herself to look at him. Later, she will say that she was struck by something in his voice. She will say: 'Is that what is meant by a toneless voice? You couldn't tell whether he was asking a question or answering it.' In kindness, she smiles and talks to him.

'Well, I must admit, actually, there aren't many, but it does happen. There was the wife of one of our own Secretaries at the Spanish Consulate; she went out of her mind. She was convinced she had contracted leprosy. Nothing would persuade her otherwise. She had to be sent home.'

Weaving in and out among the dancing couples, Charles Rossett is silent. His blue eyes—blue—are fixed, as he looks down on her hair. Suddenly, his expression changes, as though he were suffering a twinge of pain. They smile at one another, and seem on the point of speaking, but they do not.

'If no one could get used to it . . .' says the Vice-Consul. He laughs.

People are thinking: The Vice-Consul is laughing, but what a laugh! Like the sound track of a dubbed film, utterly lacking in conviction.

Once more she draws back a little and, this time, does venture to look at him.

'No, don't worry, everyone gets used to it in time.'

'But had this woman, in fact, contracted leprosy?'

87

She moves away from him and, although not looking at him, feels reassured, believing that she has at last awakened a normal response in the Vice-Consul: fear.

'Oh!' she says, 'I really ought not to have mentioned it.'

'What I mean is . . . one can't help wondering.'

She gives a little forced laugh. He, for his part, laughs outright, and the sound of it wipes the smile from her face.

'She hadn't got leprosy, I assure you. There wasn't the least trace of infection. All our staff here have regular medical checks, you know. There is nothing to fear.'

Is he listening?

'But I have no fear of leprosy,' he says, laughing.

'There are very few cases . . . I only know of one, a ball-boy. It happened after I got here, so I can assure you at first hand that the most stringent precautions were taken. . . . All the balls were incinerated, and the rackets.'

No, he is not really listening.

'You were saying that everyone, when they first come here. . . .'

'Yes, of course, but it doesn't always take the same form. Fear of leprosy carried to such lengths . . . I'm sure you understand. . . .'

Someone says:

'Did you know that if you strike a leper, he explodes like a bag of sawdust?'

'Without uttering a single cry? Without pain, perhaps? Might it not even be a great relief, an inexpressible relief?'

'Who can tell?'

'Isn't the Vice-Consul of Lahore looking thoughtful? Deep in thought, isn't he?'

'Really? I've never stopped to consider what it was that was so different about him. How very interesting!'

'He told the Club Secretary he was a virgin. What do you think of that?'

'Could that be it? Total abstinence? It's a fearful thought.'

They dance.

'You must realize,' the woman is saying in her gentle voice, 'it's hard for everyone at the beginning, in Calcutta. I myself went through a period of intense depression.' She smiles. 'It distressed my husband terribly, then little by little, day by day, I got used to it. Even when one believes it to be impossible, one gets used to it. To anything. There are worse places, you know. Singapore for one. It's abominable there, because of the extremes. . . .'

No, he is not listening. She gives up the effort of making conversation.

Wearily, they ask: What manner of man was the Vice-Consul before he went to Lahore? And what manner of man is he now that he has come here from Lahore?

Charles Rossett gets it into his head, while dancing with Anne-Marie Stretter, that the incident he witnessed near the deserted tennis courts was also witnessed by someone other than himself. Someone else, in the murky light of the summer monsoon, must have been looking across to the deserted tennis courts as the Vice-Consul went up to them. Someone who is not saying a word. Anne-Marie Stretter, perhaps.

People are saying: 'Maybe it all began in Lahore.'

People are saying:

'He was bored in Lahore. That was probably it.'

'Boredom here means a feeling of cosmic desolation, induced by the vastness of India itself. This country generates a mood of its own.'

Anne-Marie Stretter is disengaged. The Vice-Consul of Lahore approaches her, apparently with some hesitation. He takes a step or two forward, and stops. She is alone. Has she not seen him coming?

Charles Rossett sees the French Ambassador go up to the Vice-Consul of Lahore and speak to him, thus neatly preventing him from dancing with his wife. Has she noticed? Yes.

'Monsieur de H., I received your personal file last week.'

The Vice-Consul waits for him to go on.

'We'll discuss it more fully another time, but meanwhile I'd like to say. . . .'

The eyes are limpid. I am at your disposal. The Ambassador hesitates, then lays his hand on the shoulder of the Vice-Consul of Lahore, who gives a start. The Ambassador leads him up to the buffet.

People are saying: 'Did you see that? The Ambassador, our Ambassador, is an admirable man.'

'Well now, let me reassure you at once. Speaking personally, I don't set much store by formal documents. . . .

Besides, let's not get this out of proportion, there's nothing so very terrible in your file.'

The hand is withdrawn from the Vice-Consul's shoulder. The Ambassador orders two glasses of champagne. They drink. The Vice-Consul never takes his eyes off the Ambassador, who is visibly embarrassed by his scrutiny.

'Come with me.' They go together into the adjoining room. 'It's too noisy in there. . . .

'I understand, my dear fellow, that you have expressed a preference for Bombay. Is that right? . . . However, it would not be possible for you to hold the same rank in Bombay as you did in . . . Lahore. You would not be an acceptable candidate, if you see what I mean. It's too soon . . . yes . . . for the time being. On the other hand, if you were to remain here . . . you would have time on your side. India, you know, is a sink of oblivion, in which everything is swallowed up. Personally, if you are agreeable, I should like to keep you in Calcutta.'

'As you wish, your Excellency.'

The Ambassador looks surprised.

'You're willing to give up Bombay?'

'Yes.'

'To be perfectly honest, I'm relieved to hear it. There's a great demand, you see, for Bombay.'

It must seem to the Ambassador that in those watchful eyes there is something of insolence, or is it fear?

'You know,' he says, 'a career has a mysterious life of its own. The more you try to direct it, the less successful you are. You can't build a career like a house. There are innumerable openings for you as French Vice-Consul, if you see what I mean. The Lahore business is, of course, a nuisance, but if you choose to put it out of your mind, other people will forget it too. Do you understand?'

'No, your Excellency, I do not.'

The Ambassador looks as though he would be glad to escape from the Vice-Consul. No, he has thought better of it.

'Don't you feel able to settle down in Calcutta?'

'I believe I could.'

The Ambassador smiles.

'It's a little embarrassing. . . . What are we going to do with you?'

The Vice-Consul looks him straight in the eyes. Insolence, there's no other word for it, the Ambassador must be thinking.

'Perhaps I should never have come to India?'

'Perhaps. But these things can be cured . . . nervous tension . . . everything that that covers. . . . But you know that, of course?'

'No, I don't.'

The women are thinking: Really, one of us should make an effort to talk to him. The sympathy of an intelligent woman might be just what is needed to bring him out. Or even quite simply a patient listener. Maybe that's all he wants.

Once again, the Ambassador seems on the point of moving away, and once again he thinks better of it. He must stay and talk to this man tonight, this man who is looking at him with death in his eyes.

'Basically, my dear fellow, all of us, myself included, are confronted at some time with the same choice, either to go or stay. If one stays, since one can never see things as they really are, one has to . . . contrive, yes, contrive a way of looking at them, to discover how. . . .' The Vice-Consul, who has been listening attentively, says nothing. 'As to what we might find for you to do here, have you any preference? Is there anything you feel yourself especially well fitted for?'

'I can't think of anything, but I should welcome your advice.'

Maybe he has been drinking. His eyes are glazed. Has he been listening? This time, the Ambassador gives up.

'Come and see me in my office on Thursday. Would eleven o'clock suit you?' He leans closer and, looking at the ground, adds, in an undertone: 'Look here . . . think it over carefully. Weigh up the pros and cons, and if, after that, you still feel you can't trust yourself, go back to Paris.'

The Vice-Consul, with a little bow, says 'Yes.'

The Ambassador goes across to George Crawn. His manner changes completely. He talks rapidly. His eyes, suddenly, are alight with interest. Charles Rossett, seeing the Vice-Consul sidle closer, follows. They can both hear what is being said. The Ambassador is talking about shooting in Nepal. The Ambassador often goes to Nepal for the shooting. He has a passion for it. Anne-Marie never willingly goes with him.

'I've given up insisting on it . . . you know what she's like. Last time, she agreed to come in the end, but she's really only happy in the Delta.'

Charles Rossett finds himself face to face with the Vice-Consul, who remarks, with a laugh:

'Some women drive a man mad with hope. Don't you agree?' He is looking at Anne-Marie Stretter who, with a glass of champagne in her hand, is half-listening to someone who is talking to her. 'The kind who gives the impression of being dreamily afloat on a sea of indiscriminate goodwill. All the sorrows of the world wash over them in waves. And that kind of woman says: "Let them all come!" '

He's drunk, thinks Charles Rossett. The Vice-Consul laughs his characteristic silent laugh.

'Do you think it's . . . that?'

'What?'

'Do you think that is the . . . attraction?'

The Vice-Consul does not answer. Has he perhaps

forgotten what he has just said? He gives Charles Rossett a sharp look.

Charles Rossett tries to force a laugh, finds he cannot, and moves away.

Charles Rossett has asked Anne-Marie Stretter to dance again. The Vice-Consul now seems to be waiting for something. The evening is proving more and more of an ordeal for him. The strain is clearly beginning to tell. It is hard to credit that he is waiting for an opportunity to ask Anne-Marie Stretter to dance. People are beginning to ask: 'What's keeping him? Why doesn't he go?'

There are now only a dozen or so couples on the dance floor. It really is too hot for dancing. Seeing the Vice-Consul standing alone, the wife of the Spanish Consul comes up to talk to him. His response is minimal, so she goes away.

It is patently obvious to everyone, as he stands near the door, that he is waiting for something, though no one knows what.

It is Charles Rossett who gives him his opportunity. A dance has just ended. Charles Rossett, happening to find himself near the door, talks to the Vice-Consul while waiting for the next dance. Thus Anne-Marie Stretter comes face to face with the Vice-Consul. He bows. They move on to the dance floor, Anne-Marie Stretter and the man from Lahore.

The eyes of the whole of white India are now upon them.

Everyone is waiting to see what will happen. They are silent.

Everyone is still waiting. They remain silent. The spectators are beginning to lose interest.

She is perspiring slightly. The moisture on her skin is cooled by the tepid breeze created by the electric fans. But for them,

94

Calcutta would be unendurable for the whites. People are saying: 'Look at that! What a nerve!' People are saying: 'Not only is she dancing with the Vice-Consul of Lahore, she's actually going to speak to him!' People are saying: 'The Vice-Consul of Lahore is not the most recent newcomer to Calcutta. No, the most recent is that tall, fair young man with the sad blue eyes, Charles Rossett. There he is, near the buffet, watching them dancing . . . he's danced with her a good many times already. He's the one, I'm certain of it. He's the next one in line for an invitation to the house in the Delta. Look at him. He seems worried about something . . . no . . . he's not watching them now . . . it's nothing, nothing. Nothing is going to happen, nothing. . . .'

The Vice-Consul must be aware that other people are circling slowly on the dance floor, and that she is feeling the heat. He must know that he is dancing as they do in Paris, and that it is not done here. He must realize, as he leads her, that she moves a little more heavily than she should, as though resisting the movement of the dance. The Vice-Consul, who as a rule seems to notice nothing, notices this. He murmurs an apology, and slows down.

It is she who speaks first.

We know, we who are watching, that she begins by talking about the heat. She has a way of talking about the climate of Calcutta that endows the subject with a kind of intimacy. But is it really likely that she would speak to him of the summer monsoon, and that island in the mouth of the Ganges that he will never see? Who can say?

'If you only knew, you have seen nothing yet. You'll see, a fortnight from now, sleep will be impossible. One lies awake, waiting for the storms. It's so damp that, after just one night of it, the piano is out of tune. I play the piano, yes, I always have. Perhaps you do, too?'

Anne-Marie Stretter has difficulty in catching the

95

Vice-Consul's stammering reply, from which she gathers that he was made to play as a child, but since then. . . .

He falls silent. She talks to him. He remains silent.

Having told her that he played the piano as a child, and then mumbled still more indistinctly that his lessons were discontinued when he was sent away to a boarding school in the provinces, he shuts up completely. She does not ask the name or location of the school, nor does she enquire why he was sent there.

People are wondering: Would she be better pleased if he were more communicative?

One must talk. That's how it is. One must.

She herself must occasionally spend the evening talking. To whom? About what?

Have you noticed how tall he is? She only comes up to his ear. He looks well in his dinner-jacket. His bearing and fine features are deceptive. Family pride . . . the terrifying abstinence of the man from Lahore, martyred, leprous Lahore, where he took life, where he enlisted death to destroy it.

She speaks to him for the second time.

'Before this, we were in Peking. It was just before the great upheaval. People will tell you, as they told us, that Calcutta is very trying, that it's impossible to get used to the astonishing heat. Don't listen to them . . . it was just the same in Peking. No one ever talked of anything else. We were overwhelmed with good advice. Every word spoken was—how shall I put it?—the last word on the subject.'

She does not attempt this.

'The last word?'

'What I mean is this: here, too, one says the first thing that comes into one's head, and that being said, there is nothing left to say. So. . . .'

He says:

'You were in Peking, too?'

'Yes, I was there.'

'Don't try to explain. I think I understand.'

'One has to get it over as quickly as possible, at all costs. One has to face the thought of it at all costs. The need to get it over and done with prevents one from talking about other quite different things, things much more remote, but which might just as well have been said. Why not? Don't you agree?

'I could be mistaken,' she adds.

It is now his turn to speak.

The Vice-Consul, addressing Anne-Marie Stretter for the first time, speaks distinctly, but with a curiously toneless delivery, the voice pitched a fraction too high, as though he were with difficulty restraining himself from shouting.

'I am told that some people here are terrified of leprosy. The wife of one of the Secretaries at the Spanish Consulate . . . .'

'Ah! yes, I see. She was, indeed, terribly afraid of it.' She goes on: 'What did she tell you about that woman?'

'That her fears were groundless, but that, all the same, they had been forced to send her back to Spain.'

'It was not established beyond doubt that there was nothing wrong with her.'

'There was nothing wrong with her.'

She moves away from him and, this time, looks him straight in the face. He does not believe her. Does this surprise her? Has he noticed her eyes, so clear, like green pools? Her smile, yes, certainly he must have seen her smile earlier, when she was alone and unaware of being watched. Yes, without a doubt. But not her eyes, else why should he be trembling now? Is this really the first time he has seen her eyes?

'It's true, there was nothing wrong with her.'

He says nothing. It is she who speaks:

'Why do you talk of her to me?'

People are saying: 'Look, there are times when her expression is so severe that it quite alters her. Her beauty changes to. . . . It's hard to interpret. Is it an expression of ferocity or something quite different—compassion?'

'Why do you talk to me of leprosy?'

'Because I have the feeling that if I tried to say what I really want to say to you, everything would crumble into dust—' he is trembling—'for what I want to say . . . to you . . . from me to you . . . there are no words. I should fumble. . . . I should say something different from what I intended . . . one thing leads to another.'

'About yourself, or about Lahore?'

She does not, like the other woman, throw back her head to look into his face. She does not press her point. She neither asks nor encourages him to go on.

'About Lahore.'

Those who are watching them see his face light up with a glow of intense happiness, the same fire, they think, that burned up there in Lahore. They are a little frightened, without quite knowing why, for one thing is certain, he intends no harm to Madame Stretter.

'You feel you must. . . .?'

'Yes. I want you to hear what I have to say. You. Tonight.'

She darts a glance at him, so swift that he is only aware of it afterwards. He begins talking in a very low voice.

Someone says: 'He's scarcely speaking above a whisper. Look at him. . . . He seems really upset, doesn't he?'

'What I want to try and explain, then, is that afterwards, although one knows that it was oneself who was in Lahore, it seems impossible, unreal. It is I who . . . I who am talking to you now . . . who am that man. I would like you to listen to the Vice-Consul of Lahore. I am he.'

'What has he to say to me?'

'That there is nothing he can say about Lahore, nothing. And that you must understand why.'

'Because it wasn't really worth it, perhaps?'

'Oh! yes. One other thing I can tell you, if you will bear with me: Lahore was also, in a sense, hope. You do understand, don't you?'

'I think so. But I feel that there was an alternative . . . something else that you might have done, without having to go to . . . such lengths.'

"Perhaps. I can't think what. All the same, I do beg you to try and, as it were, see Lahore.'

People are saying: 'What's going on? Is he telling her the whole story? Why shouldn't he? She's the most understanding woman in Calcutta. . . ."

'It's very difficult for me to "see" it entirely,' she smiles. 'I'm a woman. . . . All I can see is a glimmer in the dark, as in a dream.'

'Try and see it in the light of day. It is eight o'clock in the morning. The Shalimar Gardens are deserted. I do not yet know of your existence, that the world holds you as well as me.'

'I am beginning to see, but only a little, a very little.'

Silence falls between them. It is noticed that there is the same expression in her eyes and his, an expression of concentration, perhaps.

'It may help you if you see the man who is waking up as a clown.'

Once more, she draws away from him a little, but she does not look at him. She is concentrating.

'In other words,' she says, 'I am not to think.'

'That's it.'

Charles Rossett supposes that they are talking about Bombay and his posting, nothing more, reluctantly as far

as she is concerned. That is why she is talking so much, keeping it up at all costs. She is wearing herself out, that much is obvious.

'I should like to hear you say that you can see the inevitability of Lahore. Please answer me.'

She does not answer.

'It is vital that you should see it, if only for an instant.'

With a tiny start, she recoils. She feels obliged to smile. He is not smiling. She too is trembling now.

'I don't know how to say . . . the word "impossible" occurs in your personal file. Is that the appropriate word in this instance?'

He is silent. She asks again:

'Is that the word? Answer me.'

'I don't know myself. Like you, I am searching for the answer.'

'Perhaps there is a better way of putting it?'

'It's not important now.'

'I can see the inevitability of Lahore,' she says. 'I could already see it yesterday, but I didn't realize it.'

That is all. For a long time neither says a word. Then, very diffidently, he asks:

'Do you think there is anything that you and I together could do to help me?'

About this, she is in no doubt.

'No, there's nothing. You have no need of anything.'

'If you say so.'

The dance is over.

It is one o'clock in the morning. She is dancing with Charles Rossett.

'What sort of man is he?'

'Oh! a dead man.'

Dead. The word escapes from pursed lips, moist lips, pale at this late hour. Is it a condemnation? He does not know. He says:

'Anyway, you talked to him. It must have done him good. It's a terrible thing to say, but I just can't stand him.'

'It's no use trying. At least, I don't think so.'

He is standing near the buffet, watching them. He is alone.

'There's no point in talking about it,' she goes on. 'It's very difficult . . . besides it's impossible to . . . I believe that if a thing is forced upon one's attention, it is sometimes because . . . a catastrophe can occur a long way from the source of the disturbance . . . you know what I mean . . . the sea, for instance, flooding inland, hundreds of miles from the subterranean explosion which causes the floods. . . .'

'Is he the catastrophe?'

'Yes. Admittedly, it's the central concept of classical drama, but none the less true for that. No need to look any further.'

She is avoiding his eyes.

'It's the best way to look at it,' she adds.

Charles Rossett thinks: She's telling the truth. Yes. I shouldn't want her to lie to me, not her.

The Vice-Consul's face is once more impassive. Look at him . . . is he . . . ? Is it desperation? She says not. She is telling the truth. She wouldn't lie.

Madame Stretter is telling the truth.

The Vice-Consul is drinking champagne. No one goes near him. It's pointless making the effort to talk to him. He never listens to anybody, everyone knows that, except to her, the wife of the Ambassador.

Charles Rossett stays at Anne-Marie Stretter's side, even after the dance is over. She is saying: 'You'll see, everything

is worth the effort you put into it here. There's music, for instance, if one has the time to spare. The only difficult thing is talking to people, and here we are, you see, talking.'

The Vice-Consul has moved closer to them, and must certainly have overheard.

She laughs. The Vice-Consul laughs too, alone. People are saying: 'Look at him now. He's moving about from one group of people to another. He's listening, but he doesn't seem to want to join in.'

The monsoon. Health precautions during the monsoon. Having to drink scalding green tea to quench one's thirst. Is the Vice-Consul waiting until she is disengaged once more? One never hears him creeping up on one. A burst of loud laughter comes from one chattering group. Someone is telling some story about a New Year's Eve party. Has anyone ever noticed that the minute one is back in France, one forgets the friends one has made in India?

They are standing at the bar. The Ambassador has joined them. They talk. They laugh. The French Vice-Consul is not far off. Some think he is waiting for a sign from them: come and join us, and that they do not wish it. It is hard on him, they think. Too hard. Others feel that he could join them if he wished, but that he prefers not to, that this is what the Vice-Consul of Lahore essentially is: a man at a distance from other men. And these people believe that he wants to keep her as she was earlier tonight, unalterably. Someone says: 'He's drinking too much. If he goes on. . . . What's he like when he's drunk?'

The wife of the Spanish Consul comes up to him for the last time. Kindly, she says: 'You look rather lost.' He does not answer, but invites her to dance.

'Far from dreading leprosy, I would welcome it,' he says. 'I lied to you just now.'

He sounds light-hearted, a little teasing. Teasing?

His eyes are wide-open, fringed with straight lashes. Not long ago his eyes were hidden by those lashes. There is laughter in his eyes.

'Why do you say that?'

'I could explain, but it would take time, and I would need an audience. I couldn't explain to just one person.'

'Oh! but why not?'

'There wouldn't be any point.'

'Oh! how sad you make it sound. Why? Don't have any more to drink.'

He does not answer.

Anne-Marie Stretter is saying to Charles Rossett:

'His voice is quite different from what one would expect from his appearance. You can't always tell what people's voices will be like just by looking at them. You can't with him.'

'It's not a pleasant voice. It's almost as though it had been grafted on to him.'

'You mean it's not his voice, but someone else's?'

'Yes, but whose?'

The Vice-Consul passes close by them. He is pale. He collapses into an armchair. He has not seen them.

It is about half past two in the morning.

'What did you talk about while you were dancing?' Charles Rossett asks.

She says:

'What did we talk about? Leprosy. He's afraid of it.'

'It's true what you said about his voice . . . but it's also true of the way he looks at one. It's as though another man were looking out of his eyes. It hadn't struck me before.'

'What other man?'

'Ah! well now. . . .'

After a moment's thought, she says:

'Perhaps one could say that his face is a blank.'

'A complete blank?'

'All but. There is an occasional flicker of expression.'

Their eyes met. The night will end, Charles Rossett thinks, with an invitation to the Islands.

She is dancing with someone else. He does not dance with anyone else. It does not occur to him.

People are saying:

'His personal file throws no light on the matter, it seems. None at all.'

'Anyway, it arrived too late to explain everything, and that includes what is in it, especially what is in it.'

'It's an odd thing, don't you think? One doesn't feel sorry for him.'

'That's true.'

'All the same, there are some men of whom one asks oneself: "What kind of woman was his mother?" '

'No, really not. Having no mother, as often as not, makes for freedom and strength of character. Actually, I'm sure he's an orphan.'

'I'm sure he'd say he was, even if he wasn't.'

'There's something I would tell you, if only I had the courage,' Charles Rossett says.

'About him?' Anne-Marie Stretter asks.

'Yes.'

'There's no point,' she says. 'Don't say anything. Don't give it another thought.'

The Vice-Consul of France in Lahore is alone once more. He has left his favourite spot near the entrance, and is standing at the bar. The wife of the Spanish Consul is no longer with him. It is now almost an hour since she left him to go into the other room. As soon as the dance was over, she went, and she has not returned. She can be heard laughing. She is tipsy.

I must go over to the Vice-Consul, thinks Charles Rossett. He means to do it. He was just going to, when the Ambassador stopped him. Charles Rossett guesses that the Ambassador has been waiting some time for a chance to speak to him. He takes his arm, and leads him to the buffet. They are not six feet from the Vice-Consul, who is drinking too much.

It is past three o'clock in the morning. Some people have already left.

People are thinking: The Vice-Consul seems to have no intention of leaving. He is quite alone. Is he always so much alone, in everyday life? Always. In his place, might not another man be drawn to seek consolation in religion? What was it about India that had turned him adrift? Had he not foreseen it before he came? Had there been no way for him to learn but by bitter experience?

The Ambassador, keeping his voice down, says:

'Look here, I dare say my wife has told you how much we would like you to spend an evening with us.' He smiles: 'You know how it is, there are some people who, more than

others, make one feel one wants to know them better. We, of course, are bound by stricter social rules than most people, but one must occasionally break them. If my wife hasn't mentioned it, it's only because she would prefer it to come from me. What do you say?'

People are thinking: If it was something in him that made him feel as he did about Lahore, was he conscious of it beforehand? Would he have come if he had known?

The Ambassador takes note of the flicker of distaste with which Charless Rossett responds to his invitation. If His Excellency is a complaisant husband, as is commonly believed in Calcutta, he must have known what I would think: Why does he go out of his way to advertise the fact? One need not jump at the invitation, declaring it to be an honour and a pleasure in store, but, at the same time, one cannot refuse the Ambassador's express request that one should go with his wife to the Islands, or keep her amused in the evenings here in Calcutta.

Some people consider it shrewd of Monsieur Stretter to deal with certain favoured newcomers in this way, clearly indicating, as they believe, the border-line which must not be overstepped later, though no one can be sure.

'I shall be happy to come.'

Anne-Marie Stretter must have a fair idea of what they are saying. She comes over to them. Charles Rossett is still, in spite of himself, a little uneasy: it's really too much, it has all happened too quickly, like cashing a post-dated cheque. He recalls something he heard at the Club: that the Ambassador had once tried his hand at writing a novel, but had given it up because his wife had advised him to do so. That was it. It was generally believed that he was resigned, but happy. Some of the things he had hoped for in life had been denied him, but he had got other things instead, things which he had not sought and was past hoping for, such as a

very young wife who, it was said, did not love him, but was prepared to join her life to his.

They are united. They have lived together in the capital cities of Asia for seventeen years. Now their active life is drawing to its close. The story goes that one day, not so long ago, she said to him: 'I don't think you should write. Let's stay here, in this part of the world, in China or in India. No one really knows what makes a poet. In any century, no more than ten poets emerge among tens of thousands of men. . . . Let's not do anything. . . . Let's just stay here . . . doing nothing.' She comes up and has a glass of champagne with them, and then goes to speak to someone who has just arrived.

The Ambassador says: 'I saw you talking to the Vice-Consul of Lahore. Thank you.'

Someone says: 'Well, well, here comes Michael Richard . . . he's arrived. Don't you know about him?'

Michael Richard is about thirty. He has style, which ensures that he is the centre of interest as soon as he comes into a room. He looks round for Anne-Marie Stretter, sees her and smiles.

Someone says: 'It's been going on for the past two years. . . . Didn't you know? . . . Everyone in Calcutta knows.'

Charles Rossett hears the wheezing voice close beside him. He has come across from the far end of the buffet. There is a glass of champagne in his hand.

'You're looking very thoughtful.'

People are saying: 'The Vice-Consul is still here. He seems determined to stick it out.'

People are thinking: Was it that he couldn't be sure of Lahore until he had seen it for himself? Oh! he was cruelly hard on the place.

Don't answer him, thinks Charles Rossett, keep your defences up. Presumably he hasn't seen Michael Richard yet.

What does it matter, anyway? What does he see? Her, apparently, nothing but her.

'I feel like some champagne,' says Charles Rossett. 'Ever since I got here, I've been drinking too much. . . .'

He is a man who inevitably arouses curiosity. Charles Rossett wishes he had the courage to ask:

'That bicycle, the woman's bicycle belonging to Madame Stretter, how do you see it?'

He knows what the reply would be:

'I have nothing to say about the reasons.'

People are thinking: And when Lahore turned out to be just as he had imagined it, he pronounced sentence of death on Lahore.

A woman says: 'I've heard the priest say that through prayer all questions are answered.' This observation causes some amusement.

'As you'll find out,' the Vice-Consul says to Charles Rossett, 'there's no novelty in being drunk here.'

They drink. Anne-Marie Stretter is in the adjoining room with George Crawn, Michael Richard and another young Englishman whom he has brought with him. From now on, right up to the end of the party, Charless Rossett will know at all times exactly where she is.

'Madame Stretter makes one feel life is worth living, don't you agree?' remarks the Vice-Consul. Charles Rossett does not wince. He does not reply. 'You will be made welcome, and saved from sin. It's no use denying it,' proceeds the Vice-Consul. 'I heard it all.'

He laughs.

Don't let him see that his shaft has struck home, thinks Charles Rossett. The Vice-Consul's tone is light-hearted. Laughingly, he goes on:

'How unfair!'

'You will be made welcome, too,' says Charles Rossett.

'Everyone in his turn. It's just the luck of the draw.'

Play possum.

'I shan't.' He is still laughing. 'Lahore alarms them. I strike a false note, listen to me. Please understand, however, that I have no complaints. Everything is fine.'

People are thinking: He only pronounced sentence of death on Lahore. He did not curse it. Had he done so, it would have been an admission that some power other than death had created it, and was therefore capable of destroying it. And at times, no doubt, it must have seemed to him that to believe even in death was too much, too abject, another misconception. At such times, no doubt, he would invoke fire and water, the tangible elements, the materials of the visible world, to wreak destruction on Lahore.

'Why do you say such things?' enquires Charles Rossett.

'What things?' the Vice-Consul asks.

'Forgive me. . . . We were talking about you just now while we were dancing . . . if you want to know. . . . You're afraid of leprosy, it seems? You needn't be. You know very well that leprosy spreads only among peoples suffering from a deficiency in diet. . . . What on earth is the matter with you?'

The Vice-Consul, with a grunt of fury, flings away his glass, which shatters. He is deathly pale. There is a silence, then he mumbles:

'I might have known they'd find something I never said to hold against me. It's appalling. . . .'

'You must be mad! There's no disgrace in being afraid of leprosy.'

'It's a lie! Who told you?'

'Madame Stretter.'

Abruptly, the Vice-Consul's mood changes. His anger subsides. He is struck by a blinding flash of something which could almost be happiness.

'People don't understand.'

Anne-Marie Stretter has returned to the octagonal room, and is distributing roses, which arrived from Nepal earlier in the day, among her women guests. There are protests . . . she should have kept them for herself. She says she has more than enough. Tomorrow, the reception rooms will be deserted, and the roses. . . . No, she does not really care for flowers. She hands them out hurriedly, a little too hurriedly, as though it were a rather tiresome chore, to be got over as quickly as possible. She is hemmed in by about a dozen women.

The look in the Vice-Consul's eyes is painful to see. It is as though he were waiting for someone to show him kindness, even perhaps love. It is time these things came to him. In the midst of a tangled confusion of sorrows, all the sorrows of the world, thinks Charles Rossett, it is as though he were suddenly claiming his share. The wife of the Spanish Consul comes up to him, with a rose in her hand.

'When Madame Stretter starts giving away her roses, it means she's had enough of us. It's a signal. But one can always pretend not to understand.'

The Vice-Consul says nothing.

The band has started up again, but a general hubbub has broken out. It is true, people are leaving. The Consul's wife is visibly the worse for drink.

'As you're in such low spirits,' she says to Jean-Marc de H., 'I'll tell you something that will amuse you. Not everyone will be leaving, there are some who will stay on. Yes, I might as well tell you, everyone knows anyway—and besides, as I'm a bit tiddly . . . these parties sometimes have a somewhat unconventional sequel. . . . Listen, when the party's over, they sometimes go. . . . Madame Stretter sometimes goes to a brothel in the town . . . the Blue Moon . . . with several Englishmen . . . those three over there . . . they

drink themselves silly. . . . I'm not making it up . . . you can ask anyone.'

She bursts out laughing, quite unaware that no one else is amused, and leaves. The Vice-Consul of France is staring at the ground. His glass of champagne is on the table, where he put it down a few minutes ago. He gives no sign of having heard.

'Do you believe her?' asks Charles Rossett.

In a corner of the octagonal room made bleak by the absence of flowers, Anne-Marie Stretter stands beside her husband, shaking hands and smiling.

'I don't think, myself, that the woman can have made it up,' Charles Rossett goes on.

Still the Vice-Consul of Lahore says nothing. He seems, all of a sudden, to realize how late it is. The adjoining room is by now almost empty. In here, there are still three couples on the dance floor. There is plenty of room now. Some of the lights are being switched off, and tables cleared.

The Vice-Consul walks away from Charles Rossett.

He goes towards Anne-Marie Stretter. What is he going to do?

People are still leaving. They converge on her from every direction. She is still standing in a corner of the octagonal room, shaking hands. She turns away to say something to her husband.

There are still a few people left in the adjoining room, too many. She glances in that direction. It seems to be worrying her a little.

The Vice-Consul, it appears, sees nothing of all this. He does not seem to realize that she is occupied, that she is bound to stay where she is, saying goodnight to her guests. He is in front of her. His presence casts a chill. People are turning round to look at him. He sees nothing. He bows. She does not understand. He stays where he is, still bowing. The

guests stare at him, some in amusement, others in fear. He raises his head and looks at her. He sees nothing but her, only her. He does not see the Ambassador's look of anguish. Forcing a smile which is more like a grimace, she says:

'If I dance with you there will be no end to it, and I don't feel like dancing any more.'

He says:

'I must insist.'

With a murmured apology to her guests, she follows him on to the floor. They dance.

'You were asked what I had said to you. You replied that we had discussed leprosy. You told a lie for my sake. You can't go back on it now. It's done.'

The man's hands are burning hot. For the first time, his voice sounds beautiful.

'You told him nothing?'

'Nothing.'

She looks towards Charles Rossett. Her eyes are full of sadness. Charles Rossett mistakenly assumes that the Vice-Consul of Lahore has been protesting to Madame Stretter because she repeated what he had said about leprosy, and this, Charles Rossett believes, is the cause of her distress.

'I was happy to lie for you,' she says.

One of the three Englishmen has come up to Charles Rossett —the timing is perfect. He is young, the young man who came in with Michael Richard. He has seen him before, on his way to play tennis. The young man seems unaware of what is happening, of the Vice-Consul's present mood.

'My name is Peter Morgan. You will stay, won't you?'

'I'm not sure yet.'

The Vice-Consul has just said something to Anne-Marie Stretter, something which makes her recoil. He tightens his hold. She breaks away. To what lengths will he go? The Ambassador, too, is watching him. He does not persist. But she looks as though she were only waiting for a chance to escape. She seems bewildered, perhaps even frightened.

'I know you,' she says. 'There's nothing more we need to know about one another. I think you may be mistaken about me. I hope not.'

'I am not mistaken.'

'I don't take life very seriously'—she tries to withdraw her hand—'that's my way. As far as I'm concerned, the things everyone says are true, completely, profoundly true.'

'It's no use trying to go back on it. It's too late now.'

There is a silence. It is she who breaks it:

'That's true.'

'You are close to me.'

'Yes.'

'Stay with me,' he begs her, 'now. What did you say?'

'Nothing that matters.'

'We are going to be separated.'

'I am close to you.'

'Yes.'

'I am closer to you tonight than to anyone else here, in India.'

People are saying: 'She has a gracious smile. He looks very composed.'

'I shall proceed as though it were possible for me to stay on here with you tonight,' says the Vice-Consul of Lahore.

'There's no hope of that.'

'No hope at all?'

'None. But there's no reason why you shouldn't pretend there is.'

'What will they do?'

'Drive you out.'

'I shall proceed as though it were possible for you to prevent it.'

'Yes. What is all this leading up to?'

'It will precipitate things.'

'Between you and me?'

'Yes, between you and me.'

'When you are outside in the street, shout at the top of your voice.'

'Yes.'

'I shall say that it is not you who are shouting. No, I shall say nothing.'

'What will happen?'

'They'll feel uncomfortable for half an hour or so. After that, they'll talk of India.'

'And then?'

'I shall play the piano.'

The dance is over. She disengages herself, and asks coldly:

'What is to become of you?'

'Don't you know?'

'You'll be sent away, a long way from Calcutta.'

'Is that what you wish?'

'Yes.'

They separate.

Anne-Marie Stretter walks rapidly past the buffet, and goes into the adjoining room. As soon as she is out of sight, the Vice-Consul of Lahore gives voice to his first cry. 'Don't leave me!' was what some people thought they heard.

Someone says: 'He's dead drunk.'

The Vice-Consul goes up to Peter Morgan and Charles Rossett.

'I shall stay here tonight, with you!' he shouts.

They behave as though they had not heard.

The Ambassador retires. In the octagonal room, three men are sprawling on chairs in a drunken sleep. A last round of drinks is served. But there are now very few people left at the tables.

'It's time you went home,' Charles Rossett says.

Peter Morgan snatches a couple of sandwiches off a tray which is being carried out. He asks the servant to leave them. He is hungry, he says.

'It's time you went home,' Peter Morgan says, in his turn.

The Vice-Consul of Lahore, it seems to them, is in an aggressive mood.

'Why?'

They avoid looking at him. They do not answer.

Then he cries out once more:

'I want to stay with you. Let me stay just this once.'

He looks them up and down. Later, they will say: 'He looked us up and down.' They will say: 'There was foam at the corners of his mouth. There were only a few of us left. All eyes were upon him. There wasn't a sound to be heard in the room when he cried out. It was a fit of rage. He must, wherever he went, have made an exhibition of himself with these sudden fits of rage, these wild bursts of fury.' People are thinking: The man is mad with rage, here, under our very eyes.

Charles Rossett will never forget the scene. The ballroom, now with so few people in it, seems vast. Lights have been turned out, tables cleared. There is menace in the air. The Vice-Consul's hour has come. He shrieks.

'Calm down,' says Charles Rossett. 'Please!'

'I'm staying here!' roars the Vice-Consul.

Charles Rossett grips him by the lapels of his dinner-jacket.

'You really are impossible.'

The Vice-Consul begs:

'Just once. Just for one night. Keep me with you for just one night.'

'It isn't possible,' Peter Morgan says. 'Forgive me, but a man of your sort is only interesting in his absence.'

The Vice-Consul breaks into wordless sobbing.

Someone exclaims: 'My God, what a mess!'

This is followed by a long silence. Then Anne-Marie Stretter comes in, followed by Michael Richard. Trembling violently, the Vice-Consul runs towards her. She does not move. The young man, Peter Morgan, grabs hold of the Vice-Consul, and marches him to the door of the octagonal room. He is not sobbing now. He goes like a lamb, almost as though he has been expecting it. Everyone watches as Peter Morgan hustles him across the garden. The sentries open the gates, the Vice-Consul goes through, and the gates shut behind him. They can still hear his cries. When they can no longer hear the Vice-Consul's cries, Anne-Marie Stretter says to Charles Rossett: 'Come with us.' Rooted to the spot, Charles Rossett stares at her. He hears someone say: 'I had the feeling that he was laughing and crying at one and the same time. What do you think?'

Charles Rossett follows Anne-Marie Stretter.

Someone recalls: He whistles 'Indiana's Song' in the grounds. The last of the guests remembers 'Indiana's Song.' 'Indiana's Song' was all he knew about India, until he came here.

Someone wonders: What can he have seen at Lahore that he had not seen already in other places? Was it the great mass of people? Or the combination of dirt and leprosy?

Or the Shalimar Gardens? Or was it that it was not until he discovered just how durable Lahore was that he became obsessed with the idea of destroying it? That must have been it. For, had it been otherwise, discovering Lahore might have killed him.

Throughout this night of plenty, she, symbol of emaciated Calcutta, squats under the lamp-post amongst the mad beggars, scratching her bald head. With vacant mind and withered heart, she waits, as always, for food. She chatters, telling some tale that no one understands.

Behind the brilliantly-lit façade of the Embassy, the music stops.

There is much to-ing and fro-ing behind the kitchen door. Here comes the food.

There is food in abundance tonight in the garbage bins behind the kitchens of the French Embassy.

In her dress of torn sacking she bolts the food at incredible speed, while ducking the slaps and blows of the mad beggars. With her mouth stuffed full of food, she laughs fit to choke.

She has eaten.

She wanders through the grounds, singing. She returns to the Ganges.

'Come with us,' says Anne-Marie Stretter.

Peter Morgan is back. The Vice-Consul must still be there at the Embassy gates. He can still be heard shouting.

There is dance music, coming from a record-player, very softly. No one is listening. There are five of them left in the room. Charles Rossett, a little apart from the rest, is standing near the door. He is listening to the outpourings of the Vice-Consul, whom he can imagine in dinner-jacket and black bow tie, hanging on to the railings. The outpourings cease. Unsteadily, the Vice-Consul begins to walk beside the Ganges, picking his way through the lepers. Everyone present, including Anne-Marie Stretter, is looking strained. They are listening. She is listening.

George Crawn's eyes—he seems to have no lashes—are stabbingly sharp. He gives the impression of being a cruel man, except when he looks at her. He is standing close to her. How long have they known one another? Since Peking, at least.

He turns to Charles Rossett:

'We sometimes go to the Blue Moon, and order a bottle of champagne. Would you care to come with us?'

'If you like.'

'Oh! I don't know that I feel like going to the Blue Moon tonight,' she says.

Try as he will, Charles Rossett cannot get the Vice-Consul out of his mind. He sees him walking beside the Ganges, stumbling over the sleeping lepers, picking himself

up, shouting, pulling some terrifying object out of his pocket, in flight, in flight.

'Listen,' says Charles Rossett.

'No, that's not him shouting now.'

They listen. That is not shouting, it is a woman singing. It is coming from the avenue. A sharp ear can detect the sound of shouting too, but much further off, beyond the end of the avenue, where the Vice-Consul must still be. A sharp ear can detect a muted chorus of shouting, far away, on the other side of the Ganges.

'Don't upset yourself. He must be home by now.'

'We haven't introduced ourselves,' says Michael Richard.

Where is he from? He does not live in Calcutta. He comes to see her, to be with her, for no other reason. To be with her is all he wants. He is not as young as he looks. He is at least thirty-five. Charles Rossett remembers having seen him before, one night at the Club. He must have been in Calcutta at least a week. There is some bond between them, Charles Rossett says to himself. Some lasting and stable bond, but they don't strike one as being in love, at least, not any longer. Yes, he remembers seeing him come in—it was well before the Vice-Consul's outburst of sobbing—and noticing his black hair and dark eyes. No one would be surprised if they were found dead in bed together one morning in a hotel in Chandernagore, after a night at the Blue Moon. If it were to happen, it would be during the summer monsoon. People would say: 'No reason at all. They simply lacked the will to live.' Charles Rossett is on the point of sitting down. No one has suggested that he should. She is watching him covertly. It is still open to him to turn down pleasant week-ends on the island, drives to Chandernagore in the evenings, to escape being thoroughly understood. If he sits down, it will be in an armchair that that other man will never occupy. For the first time, Charles Rossett finds himself admitted to the

inner sanctum of white Calcutta society. The choice is his, to sit down or to leave. She is watching him, he is quite sure. No doubt about it. He flops into the armchair.

How tired he feels, but, it must be admitted, pleasantly tired. She lowers her eyes, and stares at the ground. Very likely she knew all the time that he would stay tonight. It is done.

Peter Morgan returns.

'He'll be all right after a night's sleep,' says Peter Morgan. 'I told him not to worry, Anne-Marie. I knew you wouldn't hold it against him. He was very drunk. Someone had told him about your going to the Blue Moon, you know. He was babbling on about it. I suppose he thought he couldn't go too far with a woman who allowed herself to be seen at the Blue Moon. You can imagine. . . .'

Charles Rossett confirms that one of the guests did, in fact, say something about the Blue Moon.

'What did he say?' Anne-Marie Stretter asks Peter Morgan.

'He made a joke of it. He said: "Can you imagine the wife of the French Ambassador reflected in the mirrors of a place like the Blue Moon?" He talked about some other woman. I really can't remember.'

'There, you see,' says George Crawn, 'I told you it was being talked about in Calcutta. You don't care? That suits me.' He goes on, 'It's odd, there's something about that man that compels one to think about him.' He turns to Charles Rossett, 'I saw you talking to him. What about? India?'

'Yes. And, unless it's just his manner, I had the feeling he was leading me on, making fun. . . .'

Michael Richard, intrigued, says:

'I wanted to talk to him, but Anne-Marie stopped me. I wish I had. Oh! how I wish I had!'

'You wouldn't have been able to stand him,' Anne-Marie Stretter says.

'And you?'

With a slight shrug and a smile, she says:

'Oh! me . . . I couldn't stand him either . . . I didn't see why anyone else need get involved.'

'What did you talk about?'

'Leprosy,' says Anne-Marie Stretter.

'Nothing but leprosy? . . . How odd!'

'Yes.'

'It worries you, doesn't it?' says Michael Richard to Charles Rossett.

'It was very painful, what happened to him tonight.'

'What exactly did happen? Forgive me for asking, but I wasn't there?'

'He has . . . an obsession about being irrevocably excluded from . . . here.' Then, turning to Anne-Marie Stretter, 'I think he's wanted to meet you for a long time. . . . The way he hangs around the tennis courts every morning. . . . I can't think of any other reason. . . .'

They are all looking at her expectantly, but she gives no outward sign of interest.

'But you couldn't expect Anne-Marie . . .' says Peter Morgan.

'Naturally not.'

'What was he after, hanging about the tennis courts?' asks Peter Morgan.

'I don't know,' she says.

Her voice sounds very gentle. It is a precision instrument, like a hypodermic needle so fine that it causes no pain. She senses that Charles Rossett's eyes are riveted on her.

'He doesn't know where he's going, or what he's looking for,' she says.

'That's enough of him!' says Peter Morgan.

Twenty-four years of age. On his first visit to India. George Crawn is his closest friend.

Once more, muffled shouting can be heard coming from the banks of the Ganges. Charles Rossett gets up.

'I must go and see if he's got home all right. . . . I can't just sit here. . . . It'll only take five minutes.'

'He's probably shouting from his balcony,' says Peter Morgan.

'If he sees you,' says George Crawn, 'it will only make him more keenly aware of his failure, as you call it.'

'Take it from me, he's better left alone,' says Anne-Marie Stretter.

Charles Rossett sits down again. They have dispelled his anxiety. It was nothing . . . just nerves . . . the trying weather of the last few weeks.

'I dare say you're right.'

'He has no need of anyone.'

Peter Morgan and George Crawn have started a discussion on a subject they must often have talked of before. They are discussing the behaviour of a mad beggar-woman in Calcutta, who is always to be found where there is food.

Charles Rossett has quite given up the idea of leaving. Michael Richard, looking thoughtful, is asking Anne-Marie Stretter about the Vice-Consul. What does she think of him?

'Before I'd spoken to him, I thought, from the look in his eyes, that he was searching for something that had been lost, that he had lost . . . quite recently . . . that his time was wholly given up to this search for . . . an ideal perhaps, a wrecked ideal. Now I'm not so sure.'

'Misfortune tends to affect one that way, don't you think?'

'I don't believe,' she says, 'that the man is, well, an unfortunate. What could he have lost that would not have left some trace behind?'

'Everything, perhaps.'

'Where? In Lahore?'

'Very likely. If he had anything to lose, you can be sure he lost it in Lahore.'

'And what, by way of compensation, did he get out of Lahore?'

'Was it in the night that he sprayed the town with gunshot?'

'Oh! yes, shooting blind into the crowd?'

'Of course, by daylight one can see who one is hitting.'

'He whistles "Indiana's Song" in the gardens.'

George Crawn and Peter Morgan have their heads together. They cannot understand how it is that the beggarwoman has not contracted leprosy. She sleeps among the lepers, and wakes every morning among them, untainted, still not one of them.

Anne-Marie Stretter gets up. She seems to be listening to something.

'There's that woman,' she says to Peter Morgan, 'the one who sings in the avenue. . . . Listen. . . . One day, I really must find out. . . .!'

'You won't find anything out from her,' Peter Morgan says. 'She's quite mad.'

The singing fades in the distance.

'I must be mistaken, it can't be. Here we are, thousands of miles from Indo-China. How could she possibly have got here?'

'Did you know,' says George Crawn, 'that Peter was writing a book about that woman and the song she sings, the song of Savannakhet?'

After a little pause, Peter Morgan laughs:

'I am drunk with the sufferings of India. Aren't we all, more or less? It's impossible to talk about such suffering unless one has made it as much a part of oneself as breathing. That woman stirs my imagination. I note down my thoughts about her.'

124

'Why her, in particular?'

'Because nothing more can happen to her, not even leprosy.'

'There are many different Indias,' says Charles Rossett, with a smile, 'mine, yours, this India, that India. One can, of course, do what you are doing, or so it seems, though I can't be sure because I hardly know you, and that is to fit all these different Indias together.'

'Is the Vice-Consul's India a land of sorrows?'

'No, he hasn't even got that.'

'What, then?'

'Nothing, of course.'

'We are all used to it,' Michael Richard says. 'We are used to it. So are you. Five weeks is enough, three days is enough. After that. . . .'

'Rossett, are you still worrying about the Vice-Consul?'

'No. You were saying: after that . . .?'

'Oh! after that . . . after that . . . we are a good deal more put out by the Vice-Consul than by the famine which, at this very moment, is raging in the Malabar region. The man is mad, surely, quite simply mad?'

'When he cried out like that, one couldn't help remembering Lahore. . . . He used to go out on to the balcony at night, and cry out.'

George Crawn says: 'Anne-Marie has her own India, too, but it's not in our cocktail.'

He swoops down on her and kisses her.

'Should we be weeping here and now for the French Vice-Consul?'

'No,' says Anne-Marie Stretter.

No one else seems to have any views on the subject.

Champagne and orange squash are brought in. It is not hot. The rain can be heard beating down on Calcutta, on the palm trees. Someone asks: 'Are we going to the Blue

Moon?' No, definitely not tonight. It's too late. It's very pleasant here.

'I went back to Peking, you know,' says George Crawn. 'Oh! you were in every street. The whole place was a reminder of you, even after all this time.'

'I should tell you,' she says to Charles Rossett, 'that the Blue Moon is just an ordinary night-club. The Europeans are afraid to go there, because of the risk of leprosy, so they say it's a brothel.'

'The woman I heard it from,' Charles Rossett says, laughing, 'certainly hadn't been there herself.'

The storm is moving away.

'Were you just waiting to come to India?' she asks with a smile. 'Everybody is waiting, if not for India, then for something like it.'

Once more, Calcutta sends up a faint cry.

'It's true that, although the five weeks I've been in Calcutta haven't been easy, I have felt, in a way I don't really understand, that there was something here that I'd been waiting for. I suppose everyone feels the same.'

'Would you have preferred to be sent somewhere else?'

'Almost anywhere seemed preferable at the beginning.'

Michael Richard refuses to be deflected from the subject of the Vice-Consul.

'The word "impossible" keeps cropping up in his personal file, I believe.'

'What was impossible?'

'What did he want from you, Anne-Marie?'

Although she has been listening intently, she is unprepared for Michael Richard's question.

'Oh! he didn't make it at all clear.'

'And what if the Vice-Consul of Lahore were no more than one man among the many looking for a woman with whom he hoped to find oblivion?'

126

Was she smiling?

'What exactly does his personal file reveal?' Michael Richard asks.

'Oh!' she says, 'among other things, that he fired shots into the Shalimar Gardens at night.'

'Has he ever fired a gun in his Calcutta residence?'

Anne-Marie Stretter laughs.

'No,' she says, 'not once.'

'In Lahore, he shattered the mirrors as well.'

'At night, there are lepers in the Shalimar Gardens.'

'So there are in the day-time, in the shade of the trees.'

'Could he have been unhappy about a woman whom he had known elsewhere?'

'He claims never to have . . . Is it true?'

'I'm almost sure,' Peter Morgan says, 'that he felt obliged to do what he did because he had believed all his life that one day he would have to commit himself through action, and after that. . . .'

Smiling, she says:

'It's true that he, more than most people, I believe, felt it necessary to play a part.'

'What kind of part?'

'That of an enraged man, for instance.'

'Did he say anything about it to you?'

'Not a word,' says Anne-Marie Stretter.

'After that, as you were saying?' Michael Richard says to Peter Morgan.

'After that,' Peter Morgan goes on, 'he would have a claim on other people, a claim on their sympathy, a claim on Madame Stretter's love.'

Once more, distant Calcutta groans in its sleep.

'For the past three months,' George Crawn says with a laugh, 'you've had that same bunch of journalists guzzling your food and sleeping in your beds.'

She explains that they are stranded in Calcutta, waiting for the visas which will enable them to leave for China. They are bored to death.

'What are they going to do about making good the failure of the Malabar rice crop?'

'Nothing. There's no spirit of national unity, so nothing effective can be done.'

'Queuing for a week for a pound of rice. You must be prepared to suffer, Rossett.'

'I am quite prepared.'

'No,' says Anne-Marie, 'one thinks one is prepared, but one never is. It's always worse than one expected it to be.'

'All the same, it's strange, the number of suicides you always get among the Europeans in times of famine, though it does not affect them personally.'

'Anne-Marie, my own, dear Anne-Marie, play us some Schubert,' begs George Crawn.

'The piano is out of tune.'

'When I'm on my death-bed, I shall send for you to play Schubert to me. The piano isn't all that much out of tune, you just like to pretend it is. You make a sort of incantation of it: "The piano is out of tune. . . . It's so damp. . . ." '

'I do admit that I use it as a kind of opening gambit. There's that other one, too, about boredom.'

Charles Rossett looks at her with a smile.

'I believe I said it to you too, didn't I?'

'Yes.'

They all move to the little private sitting-room where he first saw her. He had not expected to find himself there ever again. It is a kind of sun-parlour, opening on to the garden and overlooking the tennis courts. There is an upright piano

next to the couch. Anne-Marie Stretter is playing Schubert. Michael Richard has switched off the electric fans. Suddenly, the air is pressing down on their shoulders. Charles Rossett goes out, comes back in, and sits on the steps leading down to the garden. Peter Morgan says he really must be going, and then stretches out full-length on the couch. Michael Richard, leaning on the piano, is watching Anne-Marie Stretter. George Crawn is sitting beside her, with his eyes closed. The smell of river mud drifts in. No doubt the tide has gone out. The resinous scent of the oleanders and the foul stench of the river are borne on the sluggishly circulating air, so that at times they are mingled and at times distinct.

The melody has already been introduced and repeated. Now, it has recurred for the third time. Everyone is waiting to hear it again. There. There it is

Leaning on the empty buffet in the octagonal drawing-room, George Crawn is saying: 'Yes, you take my tip, when it's very hot, drink scalding green tea. It's the only drink that really quenches thirst . . . keep off iced drinks. . . . I'll grant you green tea is bitter, acrid, but in the end one acquires a taste for it. It's the only way to beat the monsoon.'

The drunken journalists, sprawled in armchairs, toss and turn, groan, mutter a word or two, and drop off to sleep again.

Michael Richard thinks it would be a good idea to spend the weekend at the Prince of Wales. He explains to Charles Rossett that this world-famous hotel is on the same island as the Embassy villa.

They propose to leave at four o'clock this afternoon, after the siesta.

'Do come. You must see the Delta rice-fields. They're fabulous,' says Michael Richard to Charles Rossett.

They look at one another. They exchange smiles.

Come with us. Are you coming with us? Yes? I don't know.

Anne-Marie Stretter walks across the gardens with Charles Rossett. It is six o'clock. She points towards a distant patch of dazzling white light, under the lowering clouds: 'That's the Ganges Delta over there. It's a fantastic sight, great dark masses of greenery soaring into the sky.'

He says that he is happy. She does not answer. He looks at her, sees that she is very pale under her sunburn, sees that she has had too much to drink. Then her pale eyes flicker,

take on a look of panic, and suddenly he sees that they are full of tears. Yes, no doubt about it, real tears.

What is happening?

'It's nothing,' she says. 'It's coming out suddenly into the daylight. When it's foggy like this, it's a strain on the eyes.'

He promises to come back later in the day. They arrange to meet here, at this very spot, at the appointed time.

He walks in the streets of Calcutta. He is thinking about those tears. He is seeing her again as she was at the reception. He is trying to understand. He toys with several possible explanations, but does not consider them seriously. It seems to him now that those tears were there all along, all last night. The Ambassador's wife, with that absent look of hers, was holding them back, waiting for the dawn.

This is the first time he has seen day break in Calcutta. In the distance, blue palm trees. On the banks of the Ganges, lepers and dogs interspersed encircle the city. They form the wide outer ring of the city. The thousands dying of hunger are farther off to the north, in the seething bowels of the city. They form the inner ring of the city. The murky light is unlike any other. The people of the city, each after his kind, wake to endless travail.

First, the outer ring all along the banks of the Ganges, the lepers spread about in rows or in clusters. From time to time, one of them speaks. Charles Rossett has the feeling that he can see them more and more clearly, that his eyesight is growing sharper every day. Now he believes that he can see what they are made of: crumbling flesh and thin, watery blood. An army of men of straw, with no more strength than a bundle of straw, men whose heads are stuffed with straw, insensate. Charles Rossett walks on.

He turns down a road at right angles to the Ganges, to get away from the sprinkler-carts, which are moving slowly down the main avenue. He catches sight of Anne-Marie Stretter, dressed in black, strolling in the garden, looking at the ground.

It is seventeen years since she sailed slowly up the Mekong, in a slow boat with canvas awning, to Savannakhet, a large clearing in the virgin forest-land, surrounded by grey rice-fields. At night, clusters of mosquitoes on mosquito nets. He cannot, by any stretch of the imagination, picture her at twenty-two, sailing up the Mekong. He cannot picture that face as a young face. He cannot imagine the eyes of an inno-cent girl seeing what she can see now. He is walking more slowly now. It is already too hot. Gardens everywhere on this side of the town. The funereal scent of oleanders. The land of oleanders. He never wants to see those flowers again. Never. Not anywhere. He had too much to drink last night. He drinks too much. There is a dull ache in the back of his neck. His stomach is queasy. The pink oleanders melt into the pink sky at dawn. The piled-up heaps of lepers scatter and spread. He thinks of her. He tries to think of her, nothing but her: a girlish figure seated on a couch, overlooking a river. She is gazing in front of her, no, he cannot see her, she is lost in the shadows. He can only see her surroundings: the forest, the Mekong river. A crowd of about twenty people has gathered in the metalled road. She is ill. At night she weeps, and it is thought that the best thing would be to send her back to France. Her family are alarmed. They never stop talking. They talk too much, too loudly. Wrought-iron gates in the distance, sentries in khaki uniform. Already they are guarding her, as she will be guarded for the rest of her life. It would be a relief to everyone if she would give vent to her boredom in an angry outburst. It would not surprise them if she were to collapse before their eyes, but no, she is

still sitting silently on her couch when Monsieur Stretter arrives, and carries her away in his official launch. He told her: 'I shall leave you in peace. You are free to return to France whenever you wish. You have nothing to fear.' And all this, when he, he, Charles Rossett—he stops in his tracks —oh! he, at this period of Anne-Marie Stretter's life, was no more than a child.

They had to wait seventeen years for last night. Here. It was long delayed, too long.

He turns back, and follows a zig-zag course along the Ganges. The sun has risen, and its halo, the colour of rust, can be seen above the palm trees and buildings. One by one, the factory chimneys emit columns of smoke. It is suffocatingly hot already. Above the Delta, the sky is so heavy that if a cannon were fired into the clouds, it would create no breeze, but merely release an oily downpour. What a delight a breath of air would be this morning in Calcutta, but with the storm gathering, there is no hope of that. And there, in the distance, are the pilgrims. Already, once more, the lepers are resurgent, rising joyously above leprosy, in their eternal agony. And, suddenly, the Vice-Consul is there. Already, standing on the balcony of his residence in his dressing gown, he can see him coming. Too late to turn back? Too late. Charles Rossett remembers that the Vice-Consul mentioned that he suffered from a mild form of asthma, which made it impossible for him to stay in bed after the early morning sun had evaporated the humidity of the night air. He imagines he can already hear the wheezing voice saying: 'So, my dear fellow, only now on your way home, are you?'

No, he was wrong, those are not the Vice-Consul's first words.

'Do come in for a moment. A few minutes here or there can't make any difference to you. I can't sleep in this heat. What a nightmare!'

133

The voice is the expected wheezing voice. But how near is the Vice-Consul to a nervous collapse? He does not want to go in. The Vice-Consul has to plead with him.

'Please! Just for ten minutes.'

Once more he declines, saying that he is very tired. If it is about that little incident last night, there's no need to worry. No, it is not that. Please wait. I'm coming down to let you in.

Charles Rossett does not wait. He goes away, reflecting on the Vice-Consul's invitation. What could he possibly find to say to him? More lies? Too late. The Vice-Consul has caught up with him. He is tugging at his arm. Surely you can spare me ten minutes?

'Leave me alone, can't you. I have no wish to talk to you.'

The Vice-Consul lets go of his arm, and stands there staring at the ground. Then Charles Rossett takes a good look at him, and sees that he has had no sleep. Has he even tried to sleep? No, he has not. Charles Rossett sees that he is utterly worn out, though he does not know it or feel it.

'I know I'm a pest.'

'No, you're not.' Charles Rossett smiles at him. 'But why . . .? But you look very tired.'

'What was it I said?'

'I've forgotten.'

They are in his bedroom. There is a bottle of sleeping pills on his bedside table and, beside it, an open letter beginning: 'My dear Jean-Marc, my dear boy. . . .'

'When I heard about the Blue Moon business, I lost my head. . . . I didn't care what I said. . . . I felt there was no liberty I couldn't take. . . . I know. . . . I am an unpardonable blunderer . . . but . . . I wonder. . . .'

He cannot go on.

'Is that what you wanted to see me for? No, we didn't go.'

'That was partly it, yes.'

It is dark in the hallway outside. Someone can be heard polishing shoes. The Vice-Consul slams the door.

'I can't bear to hear them. I can't stand it after a sleepless night.'

'I know. Everyone feels it, just as you do.'

The Vice-Consul straightens up. He laughs. He is still playing a part. He is indefatigable.

'Is that so?'

'Yes.'

'But that wasn't why I asked you in,' he sniggers. 'I wanted to know—and you must admit that it's natural that I should—whether you had any luck with her, Rossett.'

'No.'

The Vice-Consul sits down on the bed. He does not look at Charles Rossett, who is standing over by the door. He speaks very rapidly, and there is a look of terrifying penetration in his eyes. Charles Rossett realizes that he is a little frightened. The Vice-Consul gets up from the bed, and comes towards him. He takes a step backward.

'With everything hanging in the balance, you mustn't love her, Rossett.'

'I don't see why . . . what business is it of yours?'

He still will not let him go. He pushes an armchair towards him, and begs him to be seated. He says:

'This isn't a personal matter concerning a woman who doesn't want me, you understand? I meddle in anything I choose, it's all one to me.'

He smiles, but his hands are shaking. Charles Rossett retreats still further.

'You look tired. You should try to get some sleep.'

The Vice-Consul shrugs eloquently. He knows what it means to be tired. He knows. He asks who was there, and what they talked about. Charles Rossett reels off a list of names, and says they talked about India.

'What about her? Didn't she talk of anything but India?' asks the Vice-Consul. 'Come on to the balcony. It's not quite so bad out there. These rooms are heat-traps.'

'Only about India, and, even then, she said very little.'

Anne-Marie Stretter, he says, is a beautiful woman. He considers her beautiful. What a striking face. Probably, she was less beautiful as a young woman than now. It was odd, but he could not imagine her younger, a very young woman.

Charles Rossett says nothing. He must, however, find something to say, to stem the flow of what he, too, can only describe afterwards as the Vice-Consul's ravings.

'You know,' he says, 'it seems that the Blue Moon is just an ordinary nightclub. They go there to drink champagne. It keeps open very late. That's the only reason they go there.'

The Vice-Consul is leaning on the balustrade, his chin resting on his clenched fists. His voice changes:

'Blue Moon or no Blue Moon,' he says, 'she's a woman without . . . preferences. That's what counts. You or me. . . . We can say such things to one another. I find her very . . . very attractive.'

Charles Rossett does not answer. The lights in the avenue go out.

'I made one blunder after another last night,' says the Vice-Consul. 'I want your advice. What can I do to put things right?'

'I don't know.'

'Is there nothing you can suggest?'

'I assure you, no. She is so . . . enigmatic . . . I know nothing. Take this very morning. . . .' I shouldn't be talking to him like this, Charles Rossett thinks, but there is an urgency in the Vice-Consul's manner that makes it impossible not to confide in him. 'She walked with me as far as the gates, and suddenly she was in tears, for no reason that I could see.

She didn't tell me why. . . . I really believe there's no accounting for anything she does. . . .'

The Vice-Consul, not looking at him, takes a tight grip on the balcony rail.

'You're a lucky man,' he says, 'to be able to make such a woman cry.'

'In what way?'

'I've heard it said that, for her, tears are an expression of ineffable happiness.'

Charles Rossett mumbles something. The Vice-Consul is mistaken. He is quite sure that it was not he who brought tears to Anne-Marie Stretter's eyes. The Vice-Consul gives him an indulgent smile. He is happy.

'You might mention me to her when you see her again,' he says. He laughs. 'I can't take any more, Rossett, you'll have to help me. There's no reason why you should, I realize that, but I'm at the end of my tether.'

What a liar he is, thinks Charles Rossett.

'Go to Bombay.'

Then at last Jean-Marc de H. says, in a curiously off-hand way:

'I shan't be going to Bombay now. . . . Yes, I've managed to swing that one on you.' He laughs. 'I have a sort of affection for her, that's why I'm not going to Bombay. The reason why I feel this great need to talk to you is that, for the first time in my life, I have found a woman to love.'

Charles Rossett has had as much as he can take. He cannot stand any more of it.

'I don't know . . . seeing her walking in the gardens every morning, and then, when she talked to me last night. . . . I hope I'm not boring you. . . .'

'Of course not!'

'You do see that I had to talk to you, don't you? Because I thought you would probably be seeing her before I did,

and because I . . . I'm incapable of doing anything for the time being. I don't ask much, just to see her again, like anyone else, just to be where she is, if need be, not saying a word.'

How hot it is, even as early as this. The fog scalds like steam. Charles Rossett goes back into the room, longing for escape.

'What do you say?' asks the Vice-Consul.

'There is nothing to say. You have no need of a go-between'—rising anger gives him courage—'And besides, I don't believe a word you've said.'

Standing erect, in the middle of the room, the Vice-Consul looks at the Ganges. Charles Rossett cannot see his eyes, only a twitch at the corner of his mouth, which might be a smile.

'In that case, why do you suppose I said it?'

'To convince yourself, perhaps. But to tell you the truth, I don't know. I'm sorry if I sounded unsympathetic. I'm exhausted.'

'Do you think love is just an illusion?'

Charles Rossett, almost shouting, says he is going. But he does not go. He returns to the subject of Bombay. It is unreasonable of him. He has been waiting for five weeks in such a fever of impatience, and now . . . all of a sudden. . . . The Vice-Consul suggests that they should discuss it further this evening. What about dining together at the Club? Charles Rossett says it is impossible, he is going to Nepal for a couple of days. The Vice-Consul turns to look him full in the face: 'You're lying,' he says. He begs Charles Rossett to give him his word of honour that he really is going to Nepal. Charles Rossett does so.

Nothing more happens. There is a long silence, broken only when Charles Rossett already has his hand on the door knob. Awkwardly he murmurs something about the mad woman who goes swimming in the Ganges. An odd

creature, has the Vice-Consul ever seen her? asks Charles Rossett.

'No.'

'Don't you know she's the one who sings in the avenue at night?'

'No.'

Charles Rossett goes on to say that she is around most of the time, a little further down on the river bank. She likes always to be where there are white people, it seems, just to be near them. She doesn't bother them. It's a kind of instinct . . . it's odd.

'Death in the midst of life,' says the Vice-Consul at last, 'death following but never catching up. Is that it?'

'That may be it, yes.'

They are driving along a straight road with rice-fields on either side, the rice-fields of the Delta. The light is murky, as at dusk.

Anne-Marie Stretter has fallen asleep on Michael Richard's shoulder. He has his arm round her for support. His hand is resting on hers. Charles Rossett is on her other side. Peter Morgan and George Crawn are in George Crawn's black Lancia: they passed them on the way out of Calcutta.

An immense stretch of land under water, criss-crossed by a thousand causeways. Strung like beads along all the causeways, in single file, rows of people with bare hands. The horizon is a straight line, as it was before there were trees or after the Flood. From time to time, as in other places, when they come to a patch of clear sky between storms, they can see rows of blue palm trees rising out of the water. There are people on foot, carrying sacks, pails or children, or not carrying anything. Anne-Marie Stretter sleeps with her mouth very slightly open. From time to time, her translucent eyelids part, and she sees Charles Rossett there beside her. She smiles at him, and drops off to sleep again. Michael Richard also smiles at Charles Rossett. Goodwill unites them.

She has just woken up. He takes her hand, and puts his lips to it in a long kiss. She lays her head on Charles Rossett's shoulder.

'All right?'

Thousands on the causeways, carrying their loads, laying them down, returning empty-handed. People surrounding the bare, watery spaces of the rice-fields, fields of upright stalks. People everywhere, ten thousand, a hundred thousand, crowded like grains of millet, walking along the causeways, an endless procession, continually on the move, each one with his tools of naked flesh hanging down on either side.

Weariness.

They do not talk, so as not to wake her. Besides, there is nothing left for them to say about the black junks sailing through the deep channels on the black water of the rice-fields. Every now and then they pass a seed-bed, a smooth patch of brilliant green, like painted silk. Every now and then, too, they notice a very slight speeding up of the processions on the causeways. It is a land of waters. They are on the frontier that divides water from water, fresh water from salt water, black water that, in the bays, mingles with the icy green of the ocean.

They have arranged to meet at one of the European clubs. They find the others already there. They have about another hour's drive ahead of them, someone says. They are very thirsty, but impatient to be on their way.

Peter Morgan asks after the Vice-Consul of Lahore. Charles Rossett says that he saw him this morning, and told him that he was going to spend a couple of days in Nepal. Peter Morgan makes no comment on the fact that he lied to the Vice-Consul, and the others seem agreed that he did the right thing.

They set off again. This time, Charles Rossett travels in George Crawn's car. Peter Morgan is in the back. He says that every time he sees the Delta landscape, he finds that his passion for India is even more intense than he had thought it. He too goes to sleep.

They drive through a storm, and emerge to see the palm groves of the Delta glistening under a patch of clear sky. It has been raining here, too. Beyond the palm groves, the same flat landscape.

The sea is rough. They leave their cars in a large garage near the landing stage. The bows of a launch bump against the pier. They go aboard. A wall of purple mist is moving towards the Islands. On one of them—'Look, there it is,' says Anne-Marie Stretter—there is a huge white building, overlooking a yachting basin where boats are moored: The Prince of Wales. It is a large island, with a village at the far end, very low-lying, so that the water comes right up to it. Between the village and the hotel, cutting them off from one another, is a fence of tall iron railings. Elsewhere, on the edge of the sea, in the sea, there are more fences, of wire netting, to keep out sharks.

As soon as they get there, they go down to the hotel beach to bathe. The beach is deserted. It is late, and the seas are running high. Swimming is out of the question. They have to make do with a dip, and a shower in the tepid spray of the waves. After her bathe, Anne-Marie Stretter goes to her villa, and the others to their rooms in the Prince of Wales. By the time they have changed, it is seven o'clock. They meet in the main hall of the hotel. She arrives, smiling, dressed in white. They have been waiting for her. They order drinks. The hall is over a hundred feet long. Very long, navy blue curtains are drawn over the windows. There is a dance floor at the far end. Here and there, banked with potted palms, there are bars. Most of the people in the hotel are British tourists. At this hour, there are people drinking at almost every table. Pedlars with trays of shoddy souvenirs come and go. Bottles of scent are displayed in glass cases. Leading off the hall are large, white dining-rooms, overlooking the sea. The buffet tables are piled high with grapes. Innumerable

waiters, bare-foot and wearing white gloves, circulate among the guests. The ceilings are two floors high, domed and decorated with gold paint. In the soft, golden light of the chandeliers, Anne-Marie Stretter's pale eyes glitter, as she reclines in a deep armchair. It is cool in here. They are surrounded by conspicuous luxury, luxury in depth. But tonight, owing to the bad weather, the great windows are curtained, and the new arrivals are disappointed at not being able to look out on the sea.

An English head waiter, passing by their table, assures them that the storm will be over by the time they have dined, and that tomorrow the sea will be calm.

Charles Rossett listens to them talking. They are discussing people who are not at present in Calcutta, but who are expected soon, people whom he will be meeting before long. It is all one to them whether they talk or sit in companionable silence. Talking is no effort, and silence no embarrassment. They are all tired after last night.

People are dancing at the far end of the hall, tourists on a cruise, who have just arrived from Ceylon.

They talk of Venice as it is in winter.

They have another round of drinks, and revert to the subject of the expected visitors.

Then she says she wants to go and look at the sea.

They go out to look at the sea. It is still rough, but the wind has dropped a little. The purple mist is everywhere, evenly spread, in among the palm trees and over the sea. They can hear the whistles of the launches, three blasts, a reminder to passengers that the last ferry leaves tonight at ten o'clock. The island is full of birds who have failed to reach the mainland. They noticed them on arrival, among the palms and in the mango trees, which they were stripping bare.

They have more drinks. They prefer to dine late, after

most of the other guests have left the dining room. Peter Morgan talks of the book he is writing.

'She will walk,' he says. 'I shall make a great thing of it. It will be an immensely long trek, broken up into hundreds of days of walking, all pulsating with the same rhythm, the rhythm of her footsteps. She will walk, and my words will echo the beat of her footsteps. She will follow a railway line, a road. She will leave behind her, as she goes, signposts driven into the ground bearing the names of places, Mandalay, Prome, Bassein. Facing westward, moving always towards the setting sun, she will cross the path of the sun, cross Thailand, Cambodia and Burma, plains under water, and mountain passes. She will walk for ten years, and, when she reaches Calcutta, she will stop.'

Anne-Marie Stretter says nothing.

'What about others like her?' asks Michael Richard. 'Surely, it will detract from the interest of the book to concentrate on her alone. When you talk of her, I see her surrounded by girls, other girls. I see them growing old on the journey from Thailand to the forest, and I see their youth restored in Calcutta. It may be because of what Anne-Marie has told me, but I see them in Savannakhet, in that light you were talking about, on a causeway among the rice-fields. As I see it, they are obscene, with bodies exposed, eating raw fish given to them by children who have been out fishing. As I see it, the children are frightened of them, but they only laugh. As they approach India, on the other hand, I see them as young and serious, squatting in a market place—you know, a small market place where there are a few whites. Still bathed in the light of the setting sun, they sell their new-born children.' He pauses for reflection, then goes on, 'But you could do it as a study in depth of just the one girl.'

Is Anne-Marie Stretter asleep?

'Of the youngest of the girls,' suggests George Crawn, 'the one driven out by her mother, perhaps?'

'The youngest. Your girl.'

Anne-Marie Stretter gives no sign of having heard.

'She comes to the Islands sometimes,' Michael Richard says. 'It's as though she were following her, as though she were following the whites. It's odd. She seems perfectly at home in Calcutta. I don't know if I'm imagining things, but I'm sure I've seen her once or twice swimming in the Ganges at night. What's that song she sings, Anne-Marie?'

Anne-Marie Stretter cannot answer. She is asleep.

'She sings and chatters. She holds forth meaninglessly in the midst of a profound silence. You ought perhaps to tell what she says,' George Crawn suggests. 'The least little thing amuses her. A passing dog makes her smile. At night she roams the streets. I should describe all this. I should make her do things the wrong way round: sleeping all day in the shade of the trees, here or there on the river bank. I would single out the Ganges as the scene of her final oblivion. I would say that the Ganges taught her how to lose herself. She has forgotten who she is, whether she is the child of X or Y. Her troubles are at an end.' George Crawn laughs. 'That's really why we're here. Never, never the smallest hint of trouble.'

She sleeps.

'But, that's exactly what she does,' Peter Morgan says. 'I have actually followed her. She goes in among the trees, finds something to chew, scratches the ground, laughs. She hasn't learnt a word of Hindi.'

Peter Morgan looks at Anne-Marie Stretter as she sleeps.

'She is as dirty as nature itself, it's incredible. . . . Oh! I want to dwell on that, her filth compounded of everything, and for a long time now ingrained in her skin, a component of the skin itself. I want to analyse her filth, describe what is in

it: sweat, river-mud, scraps of stale foie-gras sandwiches from your Embassy receptions, dust, tar, mangoes, fish-scales, blood, everything. I want to disgust you.'

What is the point of talking to this woman who is fast asleep?

'Meaningless utterances and profound silence,' says Michael Richard.

'In Calcutta, will she be a . . . dot at the end of a long line, the last distinguishable fact of her own life? With nothing left but sleep and hunger, no feeling, no correlation between cause and effect?'

'What he means, I think,' says Michael Richard, 'is something even more extreme. He wants to deprive her of any existence other than her existence in his mind when he is watching her. She herself is not to feel anything.'

'What is left of her in Calcutta?' asks George Crawn.

'Her laugh, drained of all colour, the word "Battambang" that she repeats incessantly, the song. Everything else has evaporated.'

'How will you trace her past, piece her madness together, distinguish between her madness and madness in general, her laugh and laughter in general, the name Battambang and Battambang the place?'

'Her dead children—because she must have had children who died—and other dead children?'

'Finally, the exchange, if that's what it was, or, to put it another way, the giving up, was not, in the long run, very different from any other exchange or surrender. And yet it did take place.'

'Perhaps she ought to be able to do something that others can't do, don't you think? In that way, she would be remembered wherever she went. Something for you to hold on to. It could be something quite trivial.'

Anne-Marie Stretter appears to be in a very deep sleep.

'I shall abandon her before madness overtakes her,' says Peter Morgan, 'that's for sure; but all the same I need to understand the nature of her madness.'

'Will she be alone in the book?' Charles Rossett asks.

'No, there will be another woman, who will be Anne-Marie Stretter.'

They turn to her.

'Oh!' she says, 'I've been asleep!'

People around them are saying that the storm has quite died down. They are in holiday mood.

They have dinner. The food is excellent. Michael Richard remarks that once one has known the Prince of Wales, one misses its comfort ever after, wherever one may find oneself.

The sky is visible through the palm trees. The moon is still hidden behind mountains of cloud. It is eleven at night. People are playing cards in the hall of the Prince of Wales. From here, the mainland is out of sight. The hotel faces the open sea. But the nearest of the islands are outlined against the sky, with lights strung out along their landing stages. A very light south wind is blowing, and the purple mist is beginning to disperse. It is now as hot as in Calcutta. The only difference is that the air here has a sharp, salty tang, redolent of oysters and seaweed. The Prince of Wales faces straight into the sea.

Michael Richard and Charles Rossett are walking in the avenue which intersects the palm grove. Anne-Marie Stretter returned home after dinner. Peter Morgan and George Crawn have hired a boat, and are cruising in the bay. Michael Richard and Charles Rossett are on their way to Anne-Marie Stretter's villa, where the others will join them when they get back from their trip.

The trapped birds squawk under the palms and in the mango trees. There are so many that the boughs bend under their weight. The mango trees are no longer bearing fruit, only these creatures of flesh and feather.

Couples are strolling here and there, in the palm grove. They loom up in the light of the tall standard lamps, sharply outlined, and disappear into darkness. The women fan themselves as they walk, with large white paper fans. They are all English-speaking. On either side of the avenue there

are bungalows with lighted windows. Michael Richard explains that they belong to the hotel. The palm grove follows the shore line, facing the sea and the islands. Behind it there are villas, it seems, and a narrow-gauge railway, independent of the hotel.

They can hear her a long way off. No doubt she plays the piano every evening here, as in Calcutta. Charles Rossett at once recognizes the Schubert piece that she played for George Crawn the night before. In a flash of white lightning he sees: Anne-Marie X, seventeen years old, tall and fragile, at the Venice Conservatoire. She is sitting her final examinations, playing the Schubert work that George Crawn likes. She is the white hope of western music. The applause is deafening. The richly dressed audience congratulate this beloved child of Venice. He thinks: who could have imagined her in India?

'Before I knew Anne-Marie,' says Michael Richard, 'I heard her playing one night in Calcutta, when I was walking in Victoria Avenue. I was very much intrigued. I didn't know who she was. I was in Calcutta as a tourist, I remember, and had no intention of staying on . . . from the very first day, I wanted to leave, and it was she, the music I heard her play, that made me decide to stay—that made it possible for me to stay in Calcutta. Several nights in succession, I stood there in Victoria Avenue, and then, one evening, I went into the grounds. The sentries let me through, all the french windows were open, and I walked straight into that room where we were last night. I was shaking, I remember.' He laughs. 'She turned round and saw me. She was surprised but not, I think, frightened. And that's how I got to know her.'

In a couple of sentences, he tells Charles Rossett how he left England for ever, and went into marine insurance in India with George Crawn and Peter Morgan. He explains

that this suits him, as it leaves him with a lot of free time. The music sounds nearer now.

Michael Richard opens a gate. They walk across a garden. A lighted porch, an open window to the right of it, a white wall. This is where the music is coming from. They stand still for a moment in the avenue of giant eucalyptus trees. Here too birds are roosting in the branches. The sound of the sea is behind them. There must be a beach nearby. The avenue and the sea form a continuous straight line. There, at the other end of the avenue, is the muffled sound of breaking waves, punctuated by silence.

'Ought we to disturb her while she's playing? Will she not mind?' asks Charles Rossett.

'I've never been quite sure, but I don't think so, not much, anyway.'

The villa is surrounded by a covered terrace, with pillars.

'Someone told me that Anne-Marie Stretter had broken with custom, and refused to hold receptions here in the summer.'

'Perfectly true,' Michael Richard says, with a smile. 'It's ours by prescriptive right now. When she's here, she sees no one but her friends.' He laughs.

The light from the window illuminates one of the ferns brought here from the octagonal ballroom, and is reflected in a pool near the door. The piano-playing stops. A shadow falls across the water of the pool.

She is there, in the half-light.

'Hello. I thought I heard you in the drive.'

She has on a black cotton housecoat. With a smile, she says she has just heard their friends' boat go past the hotel.

This must be her bedroom. It is sparsely furnished. On the piano, there is an untidy litter of sheet music. The brass bed is covered with a white counterpane. The mosquito net is raised. It looks like a snowball suspended above the bed.

The scent of citronella clings about the room. It is a clean smell.

'If you can stand the smell, it's the best thing for keeping the mosquitoes out.'

Michael Richard has sat down, and is leafing through the sheet music, looking for a piece that she used to play two years ago, but has not played since. She explains to Charles Rossett: 'This is where I sleep. I've had most of the furniture taken out. None of our furniture has been changed for thirty years. Nothing is ever changed. I prefer no furniture at all.'

Her manner is perhaps a little distant. He thinks: if this were Calcutta, and I had just arrived, this is how I should be received.

Michael Richard is still looking for the piece she used to play so much two years ago. She has no recollection of it.

'I'll show you round the house.'

Charles Rossett follows her into a large drawing-room—the furniture is covered in dustsheets—the same reproduction wall brackets and chandeliers, the same fake pillars and gold paint. She turns off the lights, and goes out.

'Something made you cry this morning,' Charles Rossett says.

She shrugs: 'Oh! it was nothing. . . .' She leads the way to a billiard room: there is nothing to see, nothing. She shows it to him, turns off the light, and goes out. As they are leaving one of the rooms, he takes her in his arms and kisses her. She does not resist. They are there in one another's arms, when suddenly—it takes him by surprise—even as he is kissing her he feels a shock of pain. It is as though his eyes were seared by a glimpse of a new but already forbidden relationship. Or as though he had loved her before, through other women, at other times, with a love. . . . What kind of love?

'We know nothing about one another. Tell me something . . .'

'I don't know why. . . .'

'I beg of you. . . .'

She says nothing. She may not even have heard. They go back to the bedroom. Michael Richard is wandering round the garden, humming. She calls him in. Had he even noticed their prolonged absence? He remarks that there are dead birds on the beach.

She leaves the room, saying: 'I'll fetch some ice. This lot is melted. During the monsoon it melts so quickly that. . . .'

The end of the sentence drifts back to them from the corridor leading off the porch. They cannot hear her now. There is silence in the bedroom. The scent of citronella obtrudes once more, a clean smell. Michael Richard is humming the melody of the Schubert piece. She comes back, carrying the ice in her bare hands. It stings. With a laugh, she drops it into the ice-bucket, and pours whisky for them.

'In years to come, you'll remember this heat,' she says to Charles Rossett. 'You will always associate it with your youth, and the time you spent in India. That's the best way to regard it, as something to look back on in after-life. It'll make all the difference, you'll see.'

She sits down, and starts talking about the other islands, all of which are wilder than this one. She reels off their names. They are mounds of alluvial deposit overgrown with trees, scarcely fit for human habitation. Michael Richard has been to some of them. Charles Rossett loses the thread of her narrative. He listens without hearing, thus discovering for the first time the Italian lilt in her voice. He looks intently at her for a long time. At last, becoming aware of this, she gives a little start of surprise and breaks off, but he goes on looking at her, until he seems to see her flesh shrivel away and, with a sense of shock, to see her, seated in Venice, a corpse with sunken eyes. Venice, where she came from, and to which she has returned, learned in the ways of suffering.

152

It is this vision of her that suddenly reminds Charles Rossett of the Vice-Consul. The vision is eclipsed. The thought of the ill-used Vice-Consul strikes like lightning, his affected voice, his feverish eyes, his terrible confession: 'I have a sort of affection for her . . . it's foolish. . . .'

Charles Rossett gets to his feet. Almost shouting, he confesses that this morning he did an abominable and inexplicable thing. It has just this minute come back to him. Word for word, he repeats the confession made to him by the Vice-Consul in the early hours of the morning, and his appeal. And he repeats what he said in reply: 'I don't believe a word you've said.'

'Now,' he says, 'it seems to me that, in spite of that phoney laugh of his, he was telling the truth . . . that, at great cost to himself, he was being sincere. . . . I can't imagine now why I spoke to him like that . . . it's terrible.'

In some embarrassment, she hears him out.

'Because,' says Michael Richard, 'you, and not he, were coming here to the Islands.'

She begs him to drop the subject of the Vice-Consul of France in Lahore. But Charles Rossett refuses to be sidetracked.

'Will you see him?' Charles Rossett asks. 'Not right away, I don't ask that, but please, I beg of you, let him come and see you. It isn't because I promised to intercede for him. No, it isn't that, but I do ask it of you.'

'No.'

Michael Richard is plainly unwilling to interfere.

'No one wants anything to do with him,' Charles Rossett says, 'no one. He's utterly alone . . . it's hell. You are the only person, I think, who does not share the . . . the embarrassment aroused by his presence . . . who does not take offence. That's why I don't understand your refusal.'

'Believe me,' she says, 'you're mistaken. He doesn't need

153

me. Even if he says he does . . . that scene last night . . . he was drunk, that's all.'

'Couldn't you look upon it as a bad dream,' Charles Rossett begs, 'no more than just the momentary hell of a nightmare? Then perhaps you could suffer his presence for a short while. . . . Surely, you could endure that much . . .?'

'No, I can't do it.'

'What, do you think . . . is his reason for wanting to see you?' asks Michael Richard, at length.

'Oh! maybe he felt I was well-disposed towards him, that I was, to some extent, indulgent. . . .'

'Oh! Anne-Marie. . . .'

Michael Richard gets up and goes to her. She waits for him with eyes lowered. He puts an arm round her, then lets it drop, and goes back to his chair.

'Listen,' he says. 'You too, Rossett. I am sure it will be better for all of us if we forget the Vice-Consul of Lahore. I can't go into the reasons for this. I can only say that we have no choice but to put him out of our minds. Otherwise,' he clenches his fists, 'we will be in grave danger of . . . at least. . . .'

'Go on.'

'Finding Anne-Marie Stretter changed beyond recognition.'

'Someone here is lying,' Charles Rossett says.

Charles Rossett resolves to go back to the Prince of Wales, and from there to Calcutta. He will not see them again. He paces up and down, and then returns to his seat without a word. She pours him a whisky, and he gulps it down.

'I'm sorry,' says Michael Richard, 'but you were so insistent.'

'Someone has just told a lie,' Charles Rossett says again.

'Forget it,' says Anne-Marie Stretter. 'And you mustn't hold it against him either.'

154

'It's not because of Lahore then?'

'No, that's not it.'

'Because of something else?'

'What?' Michael Richard asks.

'I don't understand,' she says. 'I can't see it.'

Michael Richard has moved over to the bed, and is sitting on it. She comes across to him, smoking a cigarette. She ruffles his hair, and puts her head on his shoulder.

'He's here, and he must live as best he can,' says Anne-Marie Stretter, 'and so, for that matter, must we.'

He gets up to leave, but she holds him back.

'Stop thinking about him. He'll be leaving Calcutta very soon. My husband will see to it.'

Charles Rossett turns abruptly, as the truth hits him blindingly.

'Oh! it's true,' he says, 'it's impossible, it's absolutely impossible to dwell on . . . the fact of his existence. . . . How can one possibly feel human affection of any kind for the Vice-Consul of Lahore?'

'You see,' she says, 'if I were to force myself to see him, Michael Richard would never forgive me. Nor, for that matter, would anyone else. I can only be the person I am when I am here with you by . . . frittering away my time like this . . . don't you see?'

'That's all one can do here, Anne-Marie,' says Michael Richard, with a laugh. 'There's nothing else.'

'Why should that be?' Charles Rossett asks, still not satisfied.

'For the sake of our peace of mind,' she says.

The big electric fan churns up the humid air, heavy with the scent of citronella. They stay where they are. It has grown stiflingly hot again. She gives them a drink, and then she too starts pacing the room. In the past few minutes, the roar of the sea has grown louder. She is beginning to feel

155

anxious about George Crawn and Peter Morgan. They have just decided to go out and investigate, when they hear the boat—three blasts on the horn. There will be no abatement of the heavy seas, Michael Richard explains, until the storm breaks. They will be putting in at the hotel. It's unlikely that they will be coming on here. Charles Rossett asks them if they think Peter Morgan will make a success of his novel.

'Tell me, are you as young as you look?' she asks.

They remain there, close to her, very close. Silence falls between them. This is not the first time that Charles Rossett has experienced this silence. The first time was last night, and then again after dinner tonight. It is not the silence that foreshadows a parting, nor that of people who have nothing to say. She has gone out into the garden. Charles Rossett, moved by the desire to see her, gets up, and then sits down again. She comes back, and turns the electric fan full on: 'How hot it is tonight!' She stands there in the middle of the room, in that fearful draught, with her eyes shut and her arms dangling. They look at her. She is thin in her black housecoat, her eyes are screwed up. She is no longer beautiful.

She seems to be in a state of what can only be described as unbearable well-being.

And now, the thing happens that Charles Rossett, without knowing it, has been waiting for. Has it really happened? Yes. There are the tears. They are oozing out between her eyelids and rolling down her cheeks, in very small, glistening drops. Michael Richard, without a word, gets up and turns his back on her.

It is over. The tears are dry. She has turned her head slightly, and is looking out of the window. Charles Rossett does not see. He does not want to. It is as though he were becoming anaesthetized by the spreading influence of this woman and her tears. They wait there, near her, near this woman, who has left them but will soon return.

156

Michael Richard turns round, and calls softly:

'Anne-Marie.'

She starts.

'Oh! I was in a kind of dream.' She goes on: 'You were there. . . .'

There is suffering in Michael Richard's face.

'Come here,' he says.

She goes to him as though they had really been parted; he puts his arms round her. Oh! you were there. Her voice seems suddenly to be coming from far away, very far away, from Venice. She cannot be seen, only heard. She meets someone, not Charles Rossett, not Michael Richard, a stranger. You're here! What a delightful surprise! It really is you, I'm not dreaming, you whom I hardly know. She says something that Charles Rossett cannot catch, about how biting the wind is this morning. These last words are lost before they reach this place, this island. The stranger to whom she is speaking has the ashen face of the Vice-Consul of Lahore. Charles Rossett shakes himself out of this crazy day-dream.

'You're asleep on your feet!'

She laughs. Michael Richard fondles her. She is sitting on his lap, with her legs drawn up.

'Oh! very nearly, I must admit. . . .'

'It's a strange thing, I thought I heard your voice, and it seemed to be coming from a street in Venice.'

Michael Richard puts his arms right round her—how young she looks, sitting in that ungainly, childish attitude on his knee—and kisses her with great intensity, then releases her. She goes to the window, opens it, looks out, and then lies down on the bed to rest.

Michael Richard gets up, then he too goes towards the bed, and stands there, very close to this woman. Stretched out, she seems much slighter than she normally appears. She is

flat, weightless, neatly laid out, like a corpse. Her eyes are closed, but she is very far from being asleep. Even the shape of her face is altered, different. Her features are shrunken, aged. She has suddenly become what she, as she is, would be if she were ugly. She opens her eyes, sees Michael Richard, and calls out his name: 'Ah! Michael. . . .'

He does not speak. Charles Rossett is also on his feet, standing next to Michael Richard. They both stand there, looking at her. Her long eyelids quiver, but the tears do not flow.

The roar of the sea is still there at the bottom of the garden, and the tumult of the storm, which has now broken. From her bed, as they stand looking down at her, she watches the storm through the open window. Charles Rossett just stops himself from calling out a name. Whose? Hers, no doubt. Why should he have the urge to call her by name?

He calls her name.

'I cry for no reason that I can explain. It's as though I were shot through with grief. Someone has to weep, and I seem to be the one.'

No doubt she is aware of the presence of the men from Calcutta. She lies absolutely motionless. If she were to move . . . no. She seems now to be in the grip of a sorrow so old that it is impossible any longer to weep for it.

Charles Rossett is half-aware of stretching out his hand towards her, of its being seized and laid over her eyes.

The quivering of the eyelids ceased. By the time they left, she was asleep.

The garden, shadowed by eucalyptus trees, is dark, but at the end of the drive there is light. The ocean is a green lake. The Islands can be seen in sharp outline. The birds

158

are shrieking, flying to the mainland, in a mad turmoil as usual.

As they are crossing the garden, they suddenly hear a voice raised in song. The singer is some way off, probably on the beach on the other side of the island. Yes, the island is long and narrow. Michael Richard recognizes the voice.

'It's the woman from Savannakhet,' he says. 'It really does seem that she follows her about.'

She has, indeed, arrived on the island. She comes almost every week-end during the summer monsoon, by the first boat, which brings supplies but no passengers. She crouches in a corner for a free ride. She has only arrived today. She never fails to get to the right island, by the same instinct that teaches mad elephants where to find banana groves. The façade of the great rectangular building, six hundred feet long, a patch of white dotted with electric lights: food.

They have left the garden now. Behind them, the door of the house opens. Anne-Marie Stretter comes out. She does not see them beyond the railings. She walks unhurriedly towards the beach.

'The singing must have wakened her,' says Michael Richard.

They are in sight of the sea and the beaches, intersected at intervals by the massive cement posts across which the wire netting is stretched.

She stops short of the beach. She stretches out on the ground under the trees, resting her chin on the palm of her hand, as she might if she were reading. She scoops up a handful of gravel and throws it. After a time, she stops flinging gravel and lies there, flat on her stomach, with her head resting on her folded arms.

Michael Richard wants to return to the hotel by way of the beach, but Charles Rossett prefers to go through the palm grove.

'When do you sleep?'

'During the day,' Michael Richard says, with a sad little smile. 'We have tried everything, including sleeping at night, but we prefer to sleep by day.'

They separate.

They will meet again tonight.

And again tomorrow, in Calcutta.

The lights go out in the deserted drive. By now, she must be out there, a milky shadow in the green water, swimming beyond the wire fencing designed to keep out the Delta sharks. Charles Rossett sees, in his mind's eye, the villa and its garden with no one there. He sees her swimming, floating on the water, drenched by every oncoming wave, asleep, perhaps, or weeping in the sea.

Should he go back to her? No. Is it because of her tears that she is lost to him?

Charles Rossett discovers that not only is she lost to him, but he has lost his desire for her.

He is well aware that in a short while day will break, bringing with it a crushing weariness, but for the moment he does not feel tired. He does not feel his weight as he walks, like an automaton, across the island.

He leaves the drive, turning into a side-path, and runs up against the wire fencing erected to keep marauders out.

He turns, and gropes along the fence, until at last he comes to a gate. After he has gone through it, the realization comes to him that he was frightened, absurdly frightened, of not being able to escape from this area of the island, which is fenced in for his greater protection.

He is on the other shore. The sun is still below the horizon. There are still a few minutes to go before sunrise. This is the first time he has seen India just before the break of day.

Here the sea is hemmed in by two long, narrow promontories. There are no trees, only a few bungalows. The current is not strong here. A road runs the whole length of the shore, which is muddy, and lapped by gentle waves. How beautiful the green sea is. Charles Rossett makes for the hotel, increasing the distance between himself and Anne-Marie Stretter.

The vanity of Anne-Marie Stretter.

She must now be coming out of the sea and going back to the empty house, with its doors and windows open, where, night and day, the electric fans hum above the head of the queen of Calcutta.

He stops in his tracks, arrested by the memory of Anne-Marie Stretter's tears.

He sees again Anne-Marie Stretter, rigid under the electric fan—in the heavenly rain of her tears, as the Vice-Consul might say—then suddenly the picture changes. There is something he wishes he had done. What? Oh! how he wishes he had raised his hand. . . . His hand is raised, it is lowered, it begins to stroke her face, her lips, gently at first, then more and more roughly. She bares her teeth in a painful contortion of a smile. More and more she surrenders her face to the impact of his hand, until it is wholly in his power. She is his willing victim. Slapping her face, he cries out that she must never weep again, never, never. She seems at this point to be losing her memory. No one is crying now, she says, there is nothing left that needs understanding. The

slapping continues, more and more regularly. It is close to attaining rhythmic perfection. Anne-Marie Stretter, all of a sudden, is endowed with sombre beauty. Her heaven is being torn down, but she is resigned to it. Smoothly, with marvellous grace, her head moves. It is an effortless movement, as though her head were attached to her neck by a system of carefully oiled and incomparably intricate wheels. It has become, under Charles Rossett's hand, a living instrument.

Michael Richard was watching them.

In a flamboyant halo of rust, the sun comes up out of the ocean. The glare is terrific. It brings a burning sensation to the eyes. Charles Rossett comes to himself, standing on the long shore-line of the lagoon. The sun disappears.

He walks away.

It is supposed by some that at this early hour it is possible to walk a few yards without too much discomfort from the heat, but this is not so. Oh! if there were only a breath of wind, even a hot wind, if only the air would stir just a little from time to time. . . .

Has the Vice-Consul taken his own life during the night?

Hurry! Get back to the Prince of Wales. Hurry! Get to bed, and sleep, with the shutters closed, until nightfall. Put your youth to bed, surrender it at long last to slumber.

He wonders: What is the Vice-Consul of Lahore really like?

Weariness has returned. He finds it hard to put one foot in front of the other. A hot wind blows up and fans this Mesopotamia of the Ganges. It is not much. I am still drunk, thinks Charles Rossett.

He seems to hear Anne-Marie Stretter's voice replying: 'Drunk with me.'

Behind him, on the road which borders the lagoon, he hears rapid footsteps, the patter of naked feet. He turns. He is afraid.

What is it?

What is there to be afraid of?

Someone is calling. Someone is coming towards him. A rather tall figure, very slender. There she is. It is a woman. She is bald, and looks like a dirty Buddhist nun. She waves her arms about. She laughs. Standing a few feet away from him, she is still calling to him.

She is mad. He is not deceived by her smile.

She waves towards the bay, and says just one word, the same word, over and over again. It sounds like:

'Battambang.'

This is the woman who is Peter Morgan's inspiration, the woman who may have come from Savannakhet.

He gets some loose change from his pocket, takes a step or two towards her, and stops. She must just have come out of the water. She is sopping wet, her legs are coated with glistening black mud from the shallows of the lagoon which, on this side of the island, faces the estuary. Mud, which the sea does not wash away, the mud of the Ganges. He does not go any nearer, but just stands there, with the coins in his hand. She repeats the word that sounds like 'Battambang.' Her skin is dark, leathery, her eyes sunken in nests of wrinkles, etched by the sun. Her head is covered with a brown crust, like a skull-cap. The sodden dress clings to her thin body. The unwavering smile is terrifying.

She fumbles inside her dress, between her breasts. There is something in her hand. She holds it out to him: a fish, a live fish. He does not move. She withdraws her hand, lifts the fish up so that he can see it, and bites its head off. Laughing more than ever, she chews the fish head. The decapitated fish jerks in her hand. He is terrified, nauseated,

and this seems to cause her much amusement. She advances towards him. Charles Rossett steps back. She advances further. He retreats again, but she is quicker on her feet than he is. Charles Rossett, throwing the coins on the ground, turns and runs away down the road.

Those steady, pounding footsteps behind him are hers. It is as though he were being chased by an animal. She did not stop to pick up the money. She runs fast, but he runs faster. The road is long and straight. He is still on the road that runs beside the lagoon. Hurry! Here is the Prince of Wales, with its wire fencing and palm grove, forbidden to her.

Has she stopped? Charles Rossett stops and looks round. Yes.

Sweat streams from his body, seeming to well up from within. The heat of the summer monsoon is enough to drive you mad. Your thoughts no longer cohere, they jostle, they burn out, leaving only fear, nothing else.

She is a hundred yards away from him. She has given up the chase.

He can think again.

Charles Rossett reflects that things are happening to him which he does not understand. He must leave the Islands, with their deserted roads, where such things as these lurk in wait.

Madness, I cannot stand. I can't help myself, I can't. I can't endure them looking at me out of their crazy eyes. Anything else, but not madness.

She is looking out to sea. She has forgotten him. What is there to be afraid of? Charles Rossett is smiling now. It's just that I'm tired, he thinks.

The sky clears. It is low overhead, grey streaked with orange, like a winter sunset. She is singing, the same song as before. With her mouth full of raw fish, she sings. A few moments ago, this same song woke Anne-Marie Stretter.

No doubt she can hear it now from where she is, stretched out under the trees in her drive. And this is his first recollection of the night that has just passed. Memory, like a trailing plant, gropes and comes to rest on the beggar-woman's song.

He retraces his steps. She has turned her back on him, and is making straight for the lagoon. Very, very deliberately she goes into the water, until she is completely immersed. Only her head can be seen bobbing on the water as, with intense concentration, like a buffalo, she swims in slow motion, as in a dream. Suddenly, it comes to him: she is hunting.

The day grinds on. The sun beats down on the island. Everything is exposed to the full glare of the sun. It irradiates the body of the sleeping girl, and even filters through to those who sleep in the hotel and the villas, in the sanctuary of their shadowy bedrooms.

This evening at the Club, the Vice-Consul says to the Secretary:

'Did I mention, Mr. Secretary, that although this fellow in the department store was a friend of mine, we never exchanged confidences?'

'The one who ratted on you, you mean, sir?'

'Just so. The one who told the store detective that it was I and not he who had stolen the record. Later he wrote me a letter saying: "What else could I do? My father would have beaten the life out of me, and after all, come to think of it, we weren't exactly friends. We never confided in one another." However hard I tried, I never could think of any secrets I might have shared with him. I still can't.'

'Sir, I was that stolen record.'

'What a mix-up, Mr. Secretary.'

'Let it pass, sir. Go on. My favourite is the one about Sunday with Père la Frite,' says the Secretary.

'I have no favourites,' says the Vice-Consul, 'but I agree that the story of Père la Frite's inn is probably the most touching.'

'I thought I was Père la Frite, sir.'

'No. On Sunday at Père la Frite's, Sunday slips away. It is tea-time. There is only an hour left. My mother looks at her watch. I have not opened my mouth, except for one remark. What remark was that?'

'That you were glad to be in Arras.'

'Correct, Mr. Secretary. It is February. Night is falling in

the Pas-de-Calais. I do not want cakes or chocolates, I only want to be allowed to stay there.'

'Your examination results, sir?'

'Excellent, Mr. Secretary, but we were nevertheless expelled.'

'And the Hungarian doctor?'

'I have an affection for him. He slips me the occasional five hundred franc note. I am about fifteen years old. How about you?'

'The same age, sir.'

'On Sundays,' the Vice-Consul goes on, 'there are always a number of parents who trail through the endless day with their boarder sons in tow. They are easily recognizable by their overcoats, several sizes too big, their navy blue caps, and the way they look at their mothers, who are invariably in their Sunday best.'

'What a mix-up, sir. On Sundays you went to Neuilly.'

'That's true.'

'Sir, we are drunk. Where is your father?'

'Where he chooses to be, Mr. Secretary.'

'And your mother?'

'My mother has grown beautiful during my time in Arras. The Hungarian lover leaves us alone for a moment. He paces up and down the street, frozen, he is frozen. Meanwhile, I am at it again: "Please, I beg of you, don't take me away from Arras!" The lover comes back, frozen. My mother says: "Whatever one does for one's children, too much or too little, it doesn't seem to make any difference." He agrees. There's no accounting for them. I go.'

'Where to?'

'Wherever you please, sir. What a bore it all is!'

'Precisely.'

'You have never told me why you wanted to stay on at boarding school, sir.'

He does not answer the Club Secretary's implied question. The Secretary leans forward and, because the Vice-Consul will probably not have many more days in Calcutta, makes so bold as to ask:

'And after Montfort, sir? Go on, tell me.'

'Nothing. It was fate, my mother said. I boil myself an egg in the kitchen, and no doubt I reflect, I don't remember. My mother decamps, Mr. Secretary. Standing near the piano in a blue dress, she says: "I am going to make a new life for myself, because what sort of a life could I hope for with you?" The recording engineer dies. She stays on in Brest. She dies. I have one remaining relative, an aunt who lives in the Malsherbes district. Of that, I am sure.'

'But about Lahore, sir, you haven't said a word about that. Go on, tell me.'

'Lahore? By then, I know what I am about, Mr. Secretary.'

'There's no understanding people, sir.'

'My Malsherbes aunt is looking out for a wife for me. Did I tell you that?' The Secretary says not. 'She is looking out for a suitable woman.'

'And you're quite agreeable?'

'Yes. She's looking for a woman who is not too plain, she may even be quite attractive—in evening dress. She will be called, well I can't say exactly, but Nicole, I think. Nicole Courseules would be a suitable name. There will be a confinement in the first year. A normal confinement. You see, Mr. Secretary?'

'I see, sir.'

'During her confinements, she will read—a rose-coloured reader, with rosy cheeks, reading Proust. There is terror in her eyes. When she looks at me she will be frightened, the little goose from Neuilly—the little white goose.'

'Shall you love her?'

'Tell me about the Islands, Mr. Secretary.'

The Club Secretary once more describes the hall of the Prince of Wales. It is like the deck of a luxury liner, he says, always in shadow because the sunlight barely filters through the heavy curtains. It has cool, tiled floors. There is a landing-stage where one can hire a boat and sail to the other islands. When, as now at the beginning of the summer monsoon, there are heavy storms, the island is full of birds. They weigh down the branches of the mango trees. They are prisoners on the island.

'What about your posting?' asks the Club Secretary.

'I shall hear something, I think, within the next day or two,' says the Vice-Consul.

'Have you any idea where it will be?'

'I think it will be Bombay after all. I see myself as clearly as in a photograph, reclining forever in an extended deck-chair on the beach overlooking the Sea of Oman.'

'Is that all? Have you nothing more to tell me, sir?'

'No, Mr. Secretary, nothing.'